THE HORSE OWNER'S
SURVIVAL GUIDE

THE HORSE OWNER'S
SURVIVAL GUIDE

Carolyn Henderson

SWAN·HILL
PRESS

First published in the UK in 1998
by Swan Hill Press, an imprint of Airlife Publishing Ltd

British Library Cataloguing-in-Publication Data
   A catalogue record for this book
   is available from the British Library

ISBN 1 85310 950 9

Typeset by Phoenix Typesetting, Ilkley, West Yorkshire.
Printed in England by Butler & Tanner Ltd., Frome and London.

Swan Hill Press

an imprint of Airlife Publishing Ltd
101 Longden Road, Shrewsbury, SY3 9EB, England

Contents

For my sisters, Joanna Worboys and Nichola Reynolds, with love.
'There are no problems, only solutions.'

Introduction

Keeping a horse is one of the biggest commitments you can make. It demands a huge amount of dedication, time, hard work and money – so much so that those who have no interest in horses often assume that anyone who owns one must have limitless time and a bottomless bank account.

The reality is that most horse owners are ordinary people with ordinary lives, struggling to juggle the demands of home, family and work. Whilst there are obviously a few who do not have to worry about how they are going to pay their next feed bill, or any other bill for that matter, most go without things that other people take for granted in order to pay for their horses' running costs. Owning a horse is not so much a hobby as a way of life, and the highs and lows can soar from one extreme to the other.

It is easy enough to understand why we do it when things go right, whether it be winning a competition, enjoying a long ride on a beautiful day or simply seeing a horse who is well looked after and happy. But when life becomes a series of problems – you never have enough time, you're permanently tired, your outgoings are winning the race against your income and everyone from your boss to your family makes demands you don't know how to meet – you may wonder if you've dug yourself into a hole you'll never get out of.

This book is designed to help you survive and improve the bad times and get maximum pleasure from the good ones, whether you are an owner with years of experience or a rider wondering whether taking on your first horse is a feasible or even a sensible idea. It looks at areas which often cause confusion, such as feeding, and shows you how to work out your priorities.

You cannot kid yourself that owning or looking after a horse is easy. But what is easy, unfortunately, is to get locked into your own pattern of life and way of doing things when making a few changes could make a huge difference. That is where this book comes in, because by looking at all aspects of keeping horses and sharing the experiences of owners from all walks of life, it could push you out of your rut and get you back on course to enjoying your horse. If you are still at the stage of dipping your toe in the water before you take the plunge, it will help you decide what sort of horse and what sort of system will be best for you.

The riders who have shared their experiences, both good and bad, for this book range from professionals who compete at top level with lots of animals to those who have one horse and simply enjoy riding. It makes no distinction between competitors whose walls are papered with rosettes and riders who have no plans to do anything other than look after and enjoy their horses: in the end, it is what you want to do that matters, not what you feel you ought to do. As long as you have the right horse for the job, you can both enjoy yourselves.

After all, enjoying yourself is what it is all about. The majority of us own horses because we get pleasure from looking after and riding them, not to make money from them. That does not mean that anyone who makes their living from horses does not like them, but rather that they may look on them in a different way. 'Professional' riders inevitably depend on producing horses to compete for owners and/or sponsors, buying and selling and teaching rather than on competition prize money, and though they may well develop a special affection for or bond with some animals they cannot let their hearts rule their heads.

The rest of us often do just that. How often do you meet someone who allows their riding to be channelled by their horse's talents or limitations rather than by what they want to do? As long as you get the same amount of pleasure, that is fair enough, but one of the first rules of survival is that logic and sentiment must have equal weight in your decisions if both owner and horse are to get a fair deal. By all means concentrate on dressage if that is what your horse excels at, but if you really want to show jump and your horse is a square peg in a round hole, you are both going to be unhappy and you will spend a lot of time feeling frustrated and guilty.

Guilt is one of the biggest pitfalls for the owner or would-be owner who cares about horses. The good news is that guilt is often misplaced, because we worry about things that a horse couldn't care less about. When you see magazine photographs of equine stars with not a hair out of place, and your horse has a patch of dried mud on his neck from a roll in the field and shavings in his tail from the previous night's snooze, it is easy to imagine that he is getting second-rate care.

Think again. Better still, think like a horse. He will not care that he has a collection of shavings in his tail, and given a choice between spending time in a field every day against spending twenty-three hours out of twenty-four in a stable because he is 'too valuable to turn out', he will not think twice. Part of the art of survival is sorting out priorities: in this case, brushing off mud from any areas where tack or rugs touch is essential, but brushing shavings out of tails is not. If more time spent on cosmetic touches means less time riding, do you really need to think twice about which takes priority?

At one time, every book on horses and riding was enough to give the most dedicated working owner a guilt complex. The timetable would start at 7 am with feeding, then continue at regular intervals throughout the day with quartering, exercising, grooming, tack cleaning and so on. Where you were supposed to fit in minor details such as earning your living or looking after your kids was not considered, perhaps because anyone who did not have twenty-four hours a day to devote to a horse's care would employ a groom to do it for them.

These days we are more realistic. Far fewer owners keep their horses on full livery, not only due to the cost but because looking after a horse – or at least doing part of the looking after – is an important part of getting to know him. But it is equally important not to wear yourself to a frazzle trying to do everything yourself when the other demands on your life and time mean that is impossible. Having high standards is essential, but you have to be realistic.

Teamwork must be another part of your survival plan, either by getting together with like-minded owners on the same livery yard and helping each other, or getting a willing but non-horsy partner to act as your emergency back-up. You do not have to be able to ride to learn how to bring in a horse, change his rugs and give him his tea.

Sharing and swapping skills is an essential skill for the modern horse owner, and can also be an important way of saving money. Last year we had to get our paddock fertilized and a farmer friend needed his daughter's pony clipping. Three clips can equal one fertilized field very nicely and there are, of course, endless variations on the barter theme.

No matter how disorganised you are in the rest of your life, you need to be organised about your horse-keeping. The really successful owners are those who have time and motion study down to a fine art, whilst the ones who always seem to be running round in ever decreasing circles make two journeys instead of one because they have forgotten something. Organisation is not something you can either do or not do; it might come easier to some people than others, but you can teach yourself to be more efficient.

The nice thing is that the skills and attitudes you acquire can often spill over into other parts of your life. There is no guarantee that your teenage daughter will keep her bedroom as immaculately as she keeps her horse's bed, but she might work out for herself that putting things away in the right place makes them easier to find next time she wants them . . .

Working out finances is one of the biggest headaches for most owners, but making a little go a long way is an essential skill. Most of the riders who shared their secrets for this book are ordinary people with ordinary lifestyles, but their horses lack none of the essentials. Again, it comes down to organisation and lateral thinking: for instance, buying feed and bedding in bulk between a group of owners usually means you can get a discount.

A lot of people contributed ideas to this book. They proved that horse owners are dedicated, inventive, always open to new ideas and possessed of a great sense of humour, though it is hard to work out whether those qualities are essential to start with or develop as you go along! They also proved that whilst survival might sometimes mean cutting corners, this need never compromise your horse's well-being or risk his or your safety.

If you work out how much it costs to keep the average horse in terms of time and money, the result can be pretty frightening. But if you compare that with the pleasures and challenges owning a horse can bring, there is no comparison. Wherever you live and whatever your lifestyle, this book will help you make the most of it.

Chapter 1
Horses for Courses

One of the most basic rules for survival is that the partnership between you and your horse will only work if he is the right type of horse for your lifestyle and you really like him. The two provisos might appear to be unconnected – but only if you really like a horse will you be prepared to devote time and money to him that might otherwise have gone on other things. If you like him, you will not begrudge the fact that you have to get up early to work him every day, or that he needs a new rug more than you need a new winter coat.

Whether you are an exhausted owner wondering if you are ever going to be able to juggle horse owning with other commitments, or a would-be buyer trying to work out what sort of horse would best suit you, you need to be realistic about your ability and ambitions. You may perhaps also need to be a little open-minded about what a particular type of horse is capable of; for instance, cobs and native ponies can and do compete against expensive well-bred horses at the lower levels of most disciplines and are much cheaper to keep.

It may be nice to dream of winning at Badminton or riding a Grand Prix dressage test, but it is fatal to let dreams get in the way of reality. If you know in your heart of hearts that it is more realistic to aim at riding club level or at the lower to middle levels of affiliated competition, you need a horse to match. Over-horsing yourself – buying an animal which demands more ability and time than you possess – is one of the quickest routes to misery. There are also a lot of so-called 'ordinary' horses who have far exceeded their owners' expectations, so it does not pay to be snobbish.

The general rule is that the greater the percentage of Thoroughbred blood, the less hardy the horse. A Thoroughbred or near Thoroughbred cannot live out all year round and will often need more food and cosseting than a hardier type. That is not to say that a Thoroughbred cannot be a wonderful horse to own, but he will not usually allow you as much leeway as a halfbred or cob type.

Although horses are all individuals, different breeds and types have different characteristics. Start by working out exactly what you want to do with your horse (or pony – the terms will often be interchangeable throughout this book) and then match your ambitions with the following checklist. That, and the issues raised later in this book about where and how you keep your horse, should enable you to decide what type of horse would fit into your lifestyle.

A cob can do anything! Lynn Russell rides the champion heavyweight show cob, Polaris, side-saddle.

When you make your final decision, your head must rule your heart. But relationships with horses, like relationships with people, are rarely based purely on logic. If you have an aversion to grey horses or an affinity for Arabs or Thoroughbreds, listen to your heart as long as you can honestly say that you can do the horse justice.

If you already own a horse, and everything points to the fact that you are a partnership heading for disaster, it is better for both your sakes to be brave and admit it. Your horse will never be happy with you if you are not happy with him. This does not apply purely to looks and temperament, but to ability: it is not fair to try and push a horse beyond what he is capable of.

Down to basics

All horses have accidents, injuries and illnesses, but you want to make sure that your horse stands the best possible chance of staying sound. A horse with problems costs as much to keep as one without – so whilst he does not necessarily have to win beauty contests, he should be of the make and shape to take the stresses and strains of work.

A horse with good conformation is more likely to stay sound. You will never find perfection on four legs, but glaring weaknesses often prove to be a weak link in the soundness chain. Different riders have different priorities, and what matters to one will not bother another: for instance, top event rider Ian Stark dislikes black horses because he believes they often have a doubtful temperament. And whilst a short coupled horse is often easier for the rider to balance, some show jumpers believe that a horse who is markedly short in the back will often lack the scope and the stride needed for big courses.

Conformation is dealt with in depth in *Showing to Win* and *How to Buy the Right Horse*, both by Carolyn Henderson and Lynn Russell and published by Swan Hill Press. But if you are looking for a horse who stands the best chance of staying sound and giving you a comfortable ride, the following pointers should be kept in mind. There will always be horses who break all the rules and never have a day off work, but they are the exception rather than the rule.

- A pretty or handsome head is nice to look at, but won't help to keep your horse sound. Remember that the appearance of a plain head can be enhanced by clever trimming and the right choice of bridle.
- No foot, no horse is a saying that is as relevant today as when it was first coined. Check that forefeet and hindfeet are matching pairs and that the horse's feet and limbs look as if they belong with his body. In particular, you do not want to see a cob on Thoroughbred legs – a substantial body on limbs and feet too flimsy to support it.
- Mature horses can be expected to show minor signs of wear and tear, such as splints and windgalls, but beware of a youngster with limbs belonging to a much older horse. If he cannot stand up to work at this stage, what will he be like later on? And if he has been hammered enough at an early stage to put such stress on his limbs, what will the legacies be?
- When you stand back and look at the horse, your impression should be of flowing lines, not an animal who is made up of two distinct halves. The front should match the back.
- A horse who is 'born on the bit' with a well-set on head and neck will often be easier to train than one who is not so well made. Upside down ewe necks mean that the horse cannot help but adopt a high head carriage and hollow back – but if the problem is incorrect muscle development rather than poor conformation, correct schooling can make a dramatic difference.
- A horse with the correct slope to his shoulder and pasterns will be a more comfortable ride than one where the angles are more upright. The latter usually produces a more up and down action, and whilst a 'sewing machine trot' may not be a problem in a driving animal, it can make for bone shaking under saddle.
- Good conformation is useless without a good temperament. Equally, a horse with appalling conformation and a good temperament will often give you heartache because he will not stand up to work.
- Asking people to define good temperament is a bit like asking them to define an elephant . . . which takes priority, the trunk or the ears? One rider's idea of a nice,

quiet horse will be another's definition of a boring plod, whilst a sensitive, forward going ride in one pair of hands may be 'touchy' in another.

Temperament is partly due to nature but the way the horse has been handled and ridden is usually a contributory factor. Few horses are born with aggressive temperaments, but a bold youngster may become pushy or worse if he is either allowed to get away with bossy behaviour or treated badly by a nervous or bad tempered owner.

So having defined the ground rules of a reasonably made, nice tempered animal, how do you expand them to suit your lifestyle? The following generalisations are just that, but may help to build a clearer picture of the horse for your lifestyle.

The all-rounder

If you want to do a bit of everything – hacking, dressage, show jumping and cross-country at local level and sponsored rides – then the world is your oyster. You could choose everything from a half or three-quarter-bred horse to a cob or native pony. Thoroughbreds, Arabs and Anglo-Arabs can all be versatile as long as you can meet the demands their breeding places on their owners.

Native ponies are suitable for adults as well as children. The author on Oaklands Tolling Bell (Toby) a pure-bred Connemara in the care of the Blue Cross horse protection scheme.

The dressage horse

At one time it used to be thought that you could only compete successfully in dressage if you had a flashy warmblood. Whilst warmbloods still predominate at top level, other breeds and types – including native ponies – give them a run for their money in competition up to Advanced Medium level. As long as a horse's conformation allows him to work on the bit, his paces are rhythmic and he has a temperament that works with you rather than against you, you can have a lot of fun and a lot of success.

The event horse

If you want to get beyond intermediate level, you are going to be looking at a Thoroughbred – or almost certainly a horse that is no less than seven-eighths Thoroughbred. This is purely because horses with a greater percentage of cold blood are not going to have either the speed or the stamina to cope with the demands of the modern cross-country course. You also have to take climatic conditions into account: heat and humidity have become a fact of life in Britain as well as countries like America and Australia, and research work at Britain's Animal Health Trust pointed to the 16hh – 16.2hh Thoroughbred as the horse best suited to cope with them.

You might like the idea of owning a top event horse, but would you really be happy with a horse of this calibre – and would he be happy with you?

At Pre-Novice and Novice level, there is no reason why a half-bred type cannot make its mark. At this level, there are not the same demands on stamina and speed, and balance and rhythm can be the deciding factors. A smaller horse is not necessarily at a disadvantage, though there is a minimum height limit of 15hh. Pure-bred and part-bred Arabs have competed successfully, though pure-breds are unusual in this field. However, that may be due as much to the fact that Arab enthusiasts more often have their sights set on endurance riding, Arab racing or showing, as to any lack of ability.

Horses with a percentage of pony blood mixed with Thoroughbred often have agility and the ability to find an 'extra leg' when necessary, which can make them very useful at Novice and even Intermediate event level. The combinations of Thoroughbred and either Connemara or Welsh Cob seem to work well, and there has been at least one advanced event horse whose pedigree contains a dash of Highland pony.

The show jumper

Whilst most horses can be schooled to jump round courses up to one metre – which takes you into the lower levels of affiliated show jumping – top level competition demands specialist horses. Warmbloods from jumping lines predominate, though there are plenty of Irish-bred superstars. The Americans often favour Thoroughbreds; a Thoroughbred who can take the pressure of competition can be a star in the show jumping ring as well as the eventing field.

The endurance horse

Any horse or pony, provided it is fit enough and ridden well enough, can compete in the lower levels of endurance. Twenty miles is not a lot for an animal who has achieved the basic level of 'riding club' fitness, and many can be trained for longer distances. Native breeds often do well, and many Welsh Cobs have gone on to higher levels.

When it comes to 60 and 100 mile rides, the Arab is undoubtedly supreme. His courage and stamina come to the fore and he has the speed and agility to cope with difficult terrain and racing finishes. But although it is unusual for heavier horses to get to the top, you do not have to buy an Arab if you have your sights set on long distances. Thoroughbreds, Trakehner crosses and Russian Kabardin horses have all made their mark – whilst at junior level, sisters Donna and Lucy Helme have had incredible success with Bobby, a skewbald pony who has shown many other horses with more conventional endurance pedigrees how to do it.

Endurance horses need to have a special attitude. They need to be tough, determined, and competitive, and many would say that their riders need to share similar attributes. Some of the most successful endurance horses have been those who found anything else rather boring; Joy Loyla's Hero, a 15.1hh palomino gelding of unknown breeding, was bought for £750 after she answered an advertisement in her local paper.

Chopsy, as he is affectionately known, was so naughty that she took him for long

Endurance horses come in all shapes and sizes. Joy Loyla's Hero, a team gold medallist at the World Equestrian Games, was a difficult ride when she bought him.

beach rides in a desperate attempt to settle his mind. Chopsy decided that this was what life ought to be about and quickly made his mark as an endurance horse. He carried Joy to numerous triumphs, including a gold medal at the World Equestrian Games in Stockholm.

The show horse

There is no getting away from the fact that the show horse has got to be a looker and a mover. He must also fit into a definite category; no matter how nice the horse, he will not succeed if he is not true to type. But if – like most of us – you have a limited budget and are fed up with seeing adverts for horses with telephone number prices, do some lateral thinking.

For those with a good eye for a horse, experience, ability and patience, it is still possible to find a champion in the rough at a price to match. Lynn Russell's Apollo, a champion lightweight show cob, originally came to her as an overgrown pony with a reputation for bucking off everyone who tried to ride him. She first spotted Polaris, her equally successful heavyweight, in a friend's field; the pure-bred Irish Draught was then a stallion. He also carries a side-saddle – cobs can do just about anything!

Briganoone, a top class show horse bought out of racing and produced by Kate Moore.

Briganoone, a top class small hunter, was raced on the Flat as a two- and three-year-old. His producer and rider, Kate Moore, bought him out of racing – if you are lucky, you might find another. If you have the time and the patience, a yearling or two-year-old should cost less to buy, though just as much to keep, as an older horse, and you can enjoy educating him and showing him in-hand until he is ready to start his ridden career.

Alternatively, what about showing a native pony, an Arab or a coloured horse? These can all fetch high prices, but you can still buy nice animals for under £2,000 and they are incredibly versatile. There are plenty of opportunities for showing within their specialist spheres and they can, of course, take part in lots of other activities.

Making mistakes

Saddling yourself with the wrong horse is expensive, in terms of heartache as well as money. The best way to survive the complicated process is to try and avoid making mistakes in the first place: prevention is better than cure! Here are some expert views on why things commonly go wrong.

David Hunter, former equine welfare manager for the International League for the Protection of Horses:

'A lot of people get themselves into trouble because they simply overhorse themselves. They overestimate their riding ability, can't manage a horse who perhaps has a bit of spirit and needs a sensitive, established rider and end up either frightened, or with a horse who runs rings round them.

We had many horses come to the ILPH described as unrideable, but who with correct re-schooling – and matching up with the right rider – have proved themselves to be lovely, talented animals. Unfortunately, a lot of people get carried away by unrealistic ambitions; they buy the sort of horse they would like to be able to ride rather than one who would suit them.

There's also a sort of snobbery, for want of a better word, in that a lot of people think that they have to have a big horse. They go for a powerful 16.3hh blood horse when what they really need is a 15.2hh – 16hh animal. Buying a young horse can also lead to problems if you don't have the experience to cope with one. I know it's a bit chicken and egg in that you aren't going to get the experience unless you try, but at least make sure that you have someone experienced to help you. A novice rider on a young horse can be the blind leading the blind.'

Lynn Russell, dealer and show producer:

'One of the commonest problems is people who buy horses they would like to be able to ride rather than ones their current standard of riding is actually suited to. Even if you have the money, there is no point in buying a Grand Prix dressage horse or a Grade A show jumper if you are competing at Novice level dressage or three-foot show jumping courses. You won't be able to ride the horse, he'll be totally confused and/or take the mickey and the bottom line is that you could spoil a good horse and lose a lot of money.

Horses aren't machines. A bad rider can spoil a good horse in a matter of weeks and it will take some serious re-schooling by a good rider to get it back to the level it was at. That doesn't mean that novice riders should buy unschooled horses – the last thing you want to do is have a few lessons and buy yourself a just backed four-year-old. But there is a world of difference between an older schoolmaster who has been there, seen it and done it all and a competition animal at the peak of his career.

Even schoolmasters need to be kept on the right road. They must be ridden occasionally by experienced riders who, in a nice way, can keep them up to the mark and remind them of the way things ought to be done. A lot of horses are very forgiving, but if you keep on pressing the wrong buttons you can't expect him to keep interpreting for you.

The other thing that often leads to trouble is when people insist on buying big horses because they think it makes them look good. If someone rings up and says they must have a horse that's at least 16.2hh, I always ask them how tall they are and how much they weigh. They'll often be much better off with a 16hh middleweight or a proper, quality cob.

Cobs have become incredibly popular, and rightly so. A show cob can't be more than 15.1hh, but you're getting a little powerhouse on four legs that can gallop, jump and do everything a bigger horse can do – often better. If you're not bothered about showing, one that's slightly over the height limit can be a really good buy.

It's also amazing how many "ordinary" people will buy a horse just because they think it's cheap, not because they particularly like it. I'll buy a cheap horse – but only if I'm sure someone will like it or I can sort out any problems – because that's my job. If your horse is your pleasure, it saves a lot of hassle and frustration, not to mention expense, if you cut out as many risks as possible.

My speciality is show horses, so obviously I'm looking for horses with good conformation and movement. But they must also be true to type. Hunters, hacks, cobs and riding horses are each very definite types and you can have a lovely horse that won't win because it's neither one thing nor another. In some cases, it's also got to be the right height: if it's half an inch over the height limit for its class you can forget it.

Temperament is always an important consideration. I've had, and won with, some difficult horses, but you always have to accept that they can let you down when it comes to the big occasion. For an amateur rider, even if you're determined to take on the professionals, you want a horse who works with you rather than against you.'

Ian Stark, international event rider:

'A horse has got to have that "Buy me, I'm special" look about it. It isn't that you can tell as soon as it looks over the stable door, but we all have individual preferences and you soon know if a horse is your type.

There might be some that I'm not sure about but might grow on me, and in that case I'd carry on looking at it. But if I think "I don't like that," I wouldn't even bother seeing it out.

I'm not looking for a show horse, but I don't want any major conformation faults that mean a horse would be less likely to stand up to the stresses of eventing. I don't like long pasterns or cannon bones, bad hocks or big flat feet and I'll rule out anything with any sign of a previous tendon injury.

I'm not over fussy about a horse being a 100 per cent straight mover, as long as it doesn't have any defects such as a crooked cannon bone. I don't mind a bit of dishing as long as the legs and feet are good. It doesn't have to be a flashy mover, either, because you can improve a lot with work.

By choice, I'll always buy a good Thoroughbred. A lot of people can't ride Thoroughbreds, because they're sharper, but if you get used to them it's like riding a Rolls-Royce of a horse. If they have to have anything else, I like a bit of Irish Draught – perhaps an eighth.

Ideally, I'll look for a horse standing about 16.1hh. I don't like them too big; they've got to be sharp and accurate, you're not looking for an old-fashioned chaser type. Really I'd be looking at anything from 15.3hh – 16.2hh.

If I'm looking at a four- or five-year-old I'll ride it with a view to assessing whether or not I think it will be trainable. If I thought it would take me a year to get it rideable, it would be a waste of time.

Unbroken youngsters are a bit different. You have to rely on your eye for a type and judge them on conformation and character. Temperament is always important in an event horse – I don't mind if they're a bit naughty, but they've got to be trainable.'

Richard Davison, international dressage rider and trainer:

'A good temperament is always a vital factor. It's no good having a physically superb horse that doesn't have the aptitude for the work. They've got to have heart, and be prepared to put their heart into it.

The less experienced the rider, the more important a good temperament becomes. In general, professionals can deal more easily with horses that have more difficult problems – not only because they have the experience, but because they have more time and usually the facilities to give that type of horse the programme he needs.

For instance, sometimes a horse will need two or three short sessions of work a day. We've got the indoor school, we've got extra horses if he needs to be worked in company and extra people if we need help.

If clients ask me to help them find horses, I like to sit down with them and take a realistic look at what they want to do. I like to discuss where they want to go to in the next five years and how that will fit in with their lives. Everyone would like to win a gold medal, but not everyone can be in that position – people have young families and careers at vital stages, and young riders are often away at school or university.

There will often be considerations that have nothing to do with a horse's dressage potential. With the professional, it doesn't really matter whether the horse is good in traffic or whether he's nice in the stable. My priority is whether he's going to come up with the goods in competition. But if you're dealing with a horse on your own and you fall out with him in the stable, you're not going to get on him and think he's a superstar.

It's nice to have a dressage horse with wonderful paces, but it's just part of the overall picture. There are a lot of relatively top horses that dish a bit: it's going to limit the horse in, for instance, medium trot, but there might be other factors that would put that horse in front of better movers.

Conformation is important, but there's no such thing as a perfect horse. The things that can limit a dressage horse are mechanical things, but it depends on the level you're aiming at. A Grand Prix horse who is very croup-high will find it difficult to lower; it doesn't mean he can't Piaffe, but he'll find it difficult to Piaffe in the classical way by "sitting down".'

Carol Mailer, show jumping trainer:

'It always amazes me how many people fall in love with a horse's looks and forget to ask about important things such as whether or not it's good in traffic. They see a horse that looks wonderful and decide they must have it – it's as if all their common sense goes out of the window!

A common mistake amongst more novice riders who decide they want to buy a show jumper is to look for a horse who is already jumping big tracks successfully. Whilst it's a good idea to buy a horse who already knows a bit about the job – because asking a novice to teach a novice is not really fair on either of them – you don't want a Grade A when you're competing over two foot nine courses.

Horses who are really talented at top level are not usually push-button rides and unless the rider knows what he's doing, things can soon go wrong. If you are a novice competitor hoping to go further, you're better off looking for a horse who will be happy jumping at your current level but who shows the ability to do more.'

Pony power

When you are trying to work out what would be your perfect horse, do not fall into the trap of assuming that it has to be at least 15hh – 15.2hh. Even worse, do not assume that the only 'decent' horse is an animal of at least 16.2hh. In many cases, you may actually be better off, and happier, thinking in terms of a large pony.

Ponies are not just for children. Britain's native breeds can do everything that horses can, and sometimes a whole lot more. They usually have kind temperaments, are hardy and cheap to keep and can be schooled to perform to as high a level as many horses. Even if you are tall and/or heavy, you will find that one of the larger breeds – Connemara, Dales, Fell, Highland, Welsh Section D – is so deep through the girth that it will take up your leg far better than a finer, narrower horse who is a hand bigger.

There are endless possibilities for enjoying and competing with native ponies. Apart from mountain and moorland showing and working hunter pony classes, which are open to adult riders as well as children, natives can excel in dressage, jumping and endurance riding. There are several native ponies competing successfully in dressage up to Advanced Medium level and occasional ones have won their way through to Advanced. Natives have completed some of the toughest endurance rides, and many are athletic jumpers. You may find restrictions in show jumping, where in most cases adults are restricted to animals over 14.2hh, but you will usually be able to get round them by opting to compete your pony in 'horse classes' only.

Some breeds, such as the Connemara, are more fashionable than others and you will find that prices are correspondingly higher. As always, price depends on the animal's age, conformation and standard of schooling: a five- to eight-year-old who is well made and well-schooled and is ready to go out and compete will be more expensive than an unbroken three-year-old. As a guide, you will be looking at paying £1,200 – £3,000-plus for a registered large native, depending on his ability, potential and competition record.

Each breed has its own breed society, which lays down standards on height, colour, conformation and size. If you do not want to show the pony in breed classes, it does not matter if he is overheight – you can have just as much fun with a 14.3hh Connemara as with one who meets the height requirements.

There are a few potential pitfalls to watch out for:

- If you want to show or breed from your pony, make sure that he or she is registered with the relevant breed society.
- Some showing classes have height limits. This means that you need to make sure the pony is within this and has, or is sure to get, the appropriate height certificate. Measurements are always taken with the pony's shoes off.
- Some overheight animals are basically ponies with longer legs and may not be as sturdy or capable of carrying as much weight as one who conforms to the breed standard.

Case histories

Bardsey Zodiac is a Connemara stallion who competes successfully at Advanced level dressage with his owner, Davina Cockcroft – not bad for a pony who was originally bought as a hairy four-year-old because Davina thought he might make a teaser for her Thoroughbred stud! Plenty of mare owners now use him as their first choice stallion, but at that stage the idea was that he could be used to find out if mares booked to the Cockcrofts' Thoroughbred stallions were in season.

Davina admits that she thought that if he did not work out, she could always have him gelded and sell him as a Pony Club pony. She decided to break him during a period when she had nothing else to ride, and was amazed by his natural balance and athleticism.

Like many native ponies, Bardsey Zodiac has lots of presence – that 'look at me' quality. Davina says that although he only measures just under 14.2hh, he thinks he is two hands bigger, and that he is such a little powerhouse that it feels as if you are riding a horse rather than a pony. He finds lateral work easy and shows a natural talent for Piaffe, one of the advanced movements that many 'natural' dressage horses find difficult when they reach that level of training.

Oxnead Aristocrat is a Haflinger, an Austrian breed of pony which over the past few years has gained in popularity in this country. He too is a talented performer at high level dressage and is equally at home jumping or carrying a side-saddle. His rider, Ann Birche, says that his temperament is wonderful – so much so that fellow competitors often forget that he is a stallion!

Endurance riding attracts many native pony enthusiasts. Nutcracker, a 12hh Exmoor pony, might be small but he is extremely sure-footed and has regularly shown bigger horses the way in 40 mile rides. Arddyn Crusader, a 15hh Welsh Cob, is another endurance specialist and has completed distances of up to 75 miles.

Oaklands Tolling Bell, usually known as Toby, is nicknamed The Perfect Pony by everyone who knows him. He is also proof of the wonderful work done by the Blue Cross Horse Protection Scheme, as Toby was in danger of being destroyed and was only saved when his owner was persuaded to sign him over to the Blue Cross. He arrived there as an uneducated seven-year-old; he had been broken in, but knew nothing more than 'stop' and 'go'. He had probably had some bad experiences jumping and showed a marked reluctance to go near coloured poles.

Toby, a 14.1hh grey with a wonderful temperament, good conformation and excellent paces, was given on loan to the author by the Blue Cross and spent four months doing all the sort of things he should have done as a four-year-old – hacking out alone and with other horses, learning to go forwards and to carry himself in balance. Lungeing him over poles built up his confidence and he proved to be a talented jumper. He is now being competed by fourteen-year-old Karen Carter and has won rosettes for dressage, showing, jumping and family pony classes.

Toby is deep through the girth and takes an adult rider with ease, but is equally suitable for a younger rider. He is living proof that performance animals do not have to be big horses!

Chapter 2
A Matter of Price

You have finally saved up enough money to buy a horse, but it has got to be cheap. You know that if you waited for another year or two, you would be able to afford something more expensive – but by now, you are fed up with waiting.

The scenario is a common one and one with which a lot of people will sympathise. Buying horses sometimes seems like buying houses: the longer you wait, the more impossible it seems. The other problem is that if you are also having to budget for tack, rugs and all the extra equipment you need, finances have to stretch a long way.

There are ways of buying horses relatively cheaply, or even of having a horse in your care without paying a penny, but before you go any further you have to be honest with yourself. Is it only the initial purchase price that is the stumbling block, or will you be stretching yourself beyond your limits on your normal day-to-day running costs? Have you worked out what they are? If not, put all your plans on hold and inject a little reality into your dreams.

Obviously there are ways to cut costs without compromising your horse's well-being and safety and you will find plenty of tips throughout this book. But even if you buy a horse that can live out for most of the time and is a good doer, there are certain basics that will cost the same whether you are looking at a Thoroughbred or a native type. The next chapter on different ways of keeping a horse will help you make your final decision on the horse for your lifestyle, but go through the costs chart to work out your likely spending pattern.

Do not be tempted to make false economies. For instance, you might think you could save £160 or so by not taking out insurance, but for ordinary one- or two-horse owner, insurance against veterinary fees is an essential. The only person who can afford to take a gamble is the professional with a yard full of horses – some of whom may only be there for a short time – or the owner who could pay a £3,000 bill for colic surgery without worrying about it. It may sound dramatic, but it could come down to the choice of being able to try and save your horse's life, or having to tell the vet to destroy him because you cannot afford expensive surgery and treatment.

Likewise, you may decide to save a similar amount by not having a horse vetted. Many experienced people do take this gamble – but no matter how knowledgeable you are, there are always risks. A horse who seems to be sound could have eye or heart problems undetectable to anyone but a vet. Even worse, an unscrupulous seller could be masking an unsoundness by giving the horse anti-inflammatory and pain relieving drugs. These would show up when a blood sample taken as part of the pre-purchase veterinary examination was analysed.

Having said that, it would be a mistake to assume that having a horse vetted before you buy him and insuring him for veterinary fees automatically rules out problems. See Chapter 9 on surviving disasters if you want to know the worst. However, at the end of the day, the odds are still in your favour if you minimise risks rather than simply keep your fingers crossed.

The costs detailed here prove that buying a horse is only the first part of the equation. Keeping him will soon make the purchase price seem much less expensive! The figures have been worked out on average prices across the country so yours may be slightly higher or lower.

A lot of people who keep horses will tell you that these costs are over the top. In some cases, they may be; in others, many owners simply do not realise how much they spend on their horses or what they go without in order to pay for them! And before you finally decide to go ahead and look for a reasonably cheap horse, remember that it costs just as much to keep a good horse as a bad one.

Running costs per month for one horse:
Livery on DIY basis: £40 – £80.
Shoeing: £23 – £27 (based on £35 – £40 every six weeks for a full set).
Insurance premium: £11 (based on cover for death and veterinary fees, with a sum insured of £1,000. More information on insurance is in Chapter 9.)
Bedding: £8 – £28 depending on type. See Chapter 5.
Feed: £4 – £32 depending on horse's type and workload.
Hay: £12.50 – £40 depending on type bought and amount fed.
Worming: £5.20.
Routine veterinary fees for vaccination and teeth rasping: £4.
One insurance excess over the year for first £95 of treatment following accident or illness: £8.
Saddlery and rugs repair and purchase: £21.
Lessons: £20 – £50 (based on one per fortnight).
Competition entry fees: £16 (based on two shows per month).
Transport costs: £76 for someone towing a trailer, including insurance and depreciation on trailer but not including purchase or towing vehicle costs.)

TOTAL COST PER MONTH: £248.70 – £306.20

Keeping the price down

If you have done your sums, survived the shock and worked out that you can afford to keep a horse but not to buy an expensive one in the first place, you now have to look

Buying at auction is not a game for novices. Few sales rings are as impressive as Tattersalls in Newmarket, home of specialist bloodstock sales.

at ways of keeping within your budget. Unfortunately, there are no New Year sales in the horse world!

There are four main ways of keeping the purchase price down, all with their pros and cons. The first is to buy a young horse and wait for him to grow up. The second is to buy an older animal who may be past his prime, or on the edge of it, but who can still give you lots of fun. The third is to buy at auction, where – unless it is one of the prestige sales – prices tend to be lower. A fourth option is to buy a horse with a problem, either because you think you can solve it or because you can put up with it. Finally, you have the option of taking a horse on loan, when, of course, he will not cost anything to buy.

The young horse
An unbroken youngster, which can range from a foal who has just been weaned to a three-year-old who is ready to back, will usually be cheaper than a four-year-old who is backed and ready to go on. In the long term, he will probably end up costing as much as an older horse, because you will have to keep him, worm him, have his feet trimmed

and so on just as often and at just the same cost. There may also be occasions when you get fed up of seeing other people riding and wish you had saved up for another year and bought an animal that was ready to go on.

On the other hand, a lot of people get a lot of fun – as well as a sense of achievement – in bringing on a youngster from scratch and making the right impressions (hopefully) on a clean sheet. As well as the fascination of seeing him develop and learn, there is the knowledge that unless he was mishandled to start with, any mistakes are down to you. Unfortunately, a lot of youngsters are either not taught basic manners or are allowed to run rings round their handlers, so do not assume that a lack of years is automatically synonymous with a lack of problems.

All foals are cute – but do you have the time, patience, expertise and facilities to keep and educate him?

If you and your young horse are going to survive the experience of his growing up, you need to make sure that you choose wisely, have the right environment and facilities for keeping and training him, and that you have sufficient experience and/or help from a successful trainer of young horses to make a good job of his education. It is unrealistic to say that only those experienced with young horses should take one on, because we all have to start somewhere to get that experience . . . but do not choose a sharp, sensitive, 17hh three-year-old for your first attempt.

All horses need adequate turn-out space and company, but this is particularly true of youngsters. A young horse will grow and mature, both physically and mentally, until he is five or six. He needs to be out in a field, learning his place in the hierarchy, not shut in a stable for twenty-two hours out of twenty-four. When the time comes to back him and start his education, you need a safe, enclosed area in which to work him, reliable helpers and plenty of time and patience.

If you are buying a youngster with the aim of gaining experience in breaking and schooling, pick one with an easy, sensible temperament. Although you might not want to buy a horse to sell later, it can be far better to start with an easy-going 14.2hh – 15.2hh or a large native pony than to leap straight into buying a bigger horse with more Thoroughbred blood. In any case, you will often be surprised by what a hairy cob or pony can do: if your 'project' is big enough for you, do not be surprised if you decide to keep him.

A good temperament, good basic conformation and reasonable movement are essential whatever sort of horse you are looking for. A youngster that meets these requirements should be athletic enough to cope with anything asked of him, provided, of course, you ask the right questions in the right way and at the right time. One who is badly put together will find it harder to work nicely, whilst a nervous or difficult temperament, however cheap the price tag, puts a horse firmly in the province of an experienced trainer.

The old saying that fools breed horses for wise men to ride perhaps has a ring of truth to it. The traditional rule of thumb is that it costs at least £1,500 to breed a foal and raise it to a yearling and that you can then add £1,000 for each year of its life. Many breeders find it difficult to recoup their investment, let alone make a profit, though a top quality youngster should always make a respectable price.

A nice horse is a nice horse whatever his pedigree, or lack of it, but buying a youngster of known parentage usually gives you a better idea of how he will end up. Some sellers are wildly optimistic about potential height and even type, but if you know that the mare was 14.2hh and the stallion was 15.2hh you have a pretty safe bet that their offspring will end up somewhere between the two.

Nothing is ever foolproof, though: I once bought a lovely eighteen-month-old Irish Draught cross Hanoverian gelding by a 16.2hh stallion out of a 16.1hh mare. At three, he stood 16.3hh and clearly was going to be over 17hh – I discovered, too late, that his

Hanoverian grandsire was 17.2hh and that he obviously took after him. The old nagsman's method for assessing a youngster's mature height is to drop a piece of string in a perpendicular line from the point of the elbow to the ground, then to invert it so that it runs from the elbow to above the withers. This will supposedly show you how tall the animal will finish up, but still provides only a 'guesstimate'.

Ideally, a young horse will be handled correctly from day one so that basic manners are instilled before he gets too big and pushy. Beware of owners or breeders who have a romanticised view of their horse's upbringing: 'completely unspoilt' is often a euphemism for 'I haven't done anything with him so he's a pushy little whatsit'. The opposite side of the coin is the yearling, two- or three-year-old who has been dragged round the in-hand classes at every available show until he is thoroughly fed up with the whole thing.

So what should a horse have been taught if this is your first experience of owning a youngster and you want to survive it? Basically, by the time he is weaned he should know how to lead from a headcollar, be tied up and have his feet picked up. Many people like to introduce a bit when the horse is two – or even earlier, if he is big and might otherwise learn that he can drag his handler around.

If you buy a yearling and want to map out his education, you could introduce a little long reining when he is three or even earlier; well-grown two-year-olds who start looking for mischief often respond to short long-reining sessions, but avoid lungeing at this stage. Circle work puts too much stress on immature joints, particularly the hocks.

CASE HISTORY:

Sonia Windsor has always been a cob enthusiast and her dream was to own a county level show cob. As 'made' animals can fetch five figures, she had to do a bit of lateral thinking and decided to buy the best youngster she could find in her price range.

Sonia eventually found Sirius, a liver chestnut three-year-old who had just been backed, in show producer and dealer Lynn Russell's yard. 'I paid what I could afford, which wasn't much!' she recalled. Three years later, Sirius is very successful in amateur owner/rider classes at county level and has also been placed in open classes against horses produced and ridden by professionals.

Sonia has regular lessons, but does all the hard work and preparation herself. She deliberately bought a horse with a nice temperament, and her long-term strategy has paid off.

The older horse

Horses are usually at their most expensive when they are between five and eight years old, provided they have been schooled correctly. In this bracket, they are old enough to have learned the basics and to have gained a bit of experience, but can still be classed

This mare was bought out of racing in poor condition and went on to make a successful riding horse.

as young animals. Endurance horses and dressage horses usually reach the peak of their careers later; Jill Thomas's Egyptian Khalifa completed his tenth Golden Horseshoe Ride, a total of 1,000 miles in this competition alone, at the age of seventeen.

As far as the 'ordinary' horse is concerned, his market value usually starts to drop once he reaches the age of ten or eleven. This will not necessarily make him cheap, but it will often mean he will cost less than he did a few years previously. A horse in his early to mid-teens who has been well looked after can give a lot of fun, provided that he is sound and that you accept that you are likely to be faced with the final responsibility for him.

Sadly, there are people who will sell an old horse for whatever they can get for him without a thought for his future. Equally, there are many caring owners who appreciate that a horse in his late teens can enjoy life in a slower lane and will find him a suitable loan home. The fact remains, though, that if you buy a horse in his teens the odds are that eventually you will be faced with the decision of either retiring him – if you can provide him with sufficient quality of life – or having him put down, which can sometimes be the kinder option.

Ponies often work happily into their mid-twenties and a wise old pony who has been there, seen it and done it all will always be in demand. But whether you are looking at a pony or a horse, you have to accept that an older animal will inevitably show more signs of wear and tear than a younger one. We all get stiffer as we get older!

Buying at auction

On the Continent, and in the racing world, buying at auction is the accepted way of doing business. In Britain, auctions have long held the image of places for getting rid of dodgy animals – and it has to be said that problem horses often end up going through the sales ring.

However, auctioneers have done a lot over the past ten years to try and make sure that buyers and sellers get a fair deal. If you do your homework, there is no reason why you should not make a good buy, as prices tend to be lower. The exceptions are the prestige sales for top class competition animals and youngstock, but even here you can sometimes find a bargain.

So how do you survive the auction experience? The main essentials are common sense, a cool head and the knowledge that no matter how careful you are, you can still make a mistake. Having said that, the same applies to buying direct.

The disadvantages of buying at auction are that you usually only get a chance to see the horse once, in sale surroundings. The impression you get from seeing an animal on his home ground is more reliable. Against this, some people feel that it is actually an advantage to see how he behaves in a strange place, and that a horse who is bold and interested but stays calm is the one to bid for.

Many sales are held at venues where you can ride the horses, but the trial will be limited to either an indoor arena or an enclosed outdoor area. You may be able to jump him, and can see how he behaves in company if other horses are being tried at the same time, but will not be able to ride him on the roads – so unless he is warranted in the catalogue as being quiet in traffic, you will have to take a gamble. In any case, one person's definition of being quiet in traffic may not be the same as another's.

The golden rules for buying at a sale are:

- Read the terms and conditions of sale. In most cases, horses which weave, crib bite or windsuck have to be described as such in the catalogue, but box walking and expensive habits such as rug chewing are not 'declarable vices.'

    If the horse is warranted as sound, make sure you understand the definition. Most terms and conditions state it as being sound in wind, eyes, heart and action, but there are occasionally slight variations. If the warranty covers wind, eyes and action, you have no comeback if you get a horse home and discover that it has a heart murmur.
- If the horse is sold sound, 'subject to re-examination,' this means that you have the opportunity to have him examined by a vet at the sale, appointed for the job

by the auctioneers. Do not make the mistake of thinking that you can take the horse home and get your own vet to do the job – if you do not have him examined there, you will be deemed to have agreed that the horse was sound when sold. You may still be able to take action if you can prove that the horse has a condition which contravenes the sale terms and was in existence when he was sold, but taking legal action could be a long, complicated and expensive business.

- Read the catalogue descriptions carefully, as much to work out what is not said as to see what is. For instance, if a horse is described as 'good to box, clip, catch and shoe,' he will perhaps be unreliable in traffic. If not, the vendor would surely have included this, as it is such an important selling point.

- Descriptions of colour, height and even age are not always guaranteed under the terms and conditions. Obviously you can look at a horse and make up your own mind, but if you are looking for an animal where height is vital – for instance, a jumping pony or a show horse on whom height limits are imposed – you may have to keep your fingers crossed. If your potential small hunter turns out to be half an inch over the 15.2hh height limit, are you prepared to sell him again? And if you do, can you be sure of getting back what you paid?

  Whilst it is easy enough to tell the age of a horse up to seven years by his teeth, things become more difficult after that. It takes a real expert to tell the difference between a ten-year-old and a thirteen-year-old, and even then it is a case of keeping your fingers crossed. The bottom line is to be careful of horses of eight years of age or over who do not have registration papers to back up their quoted ages.

- Do not get carried away by the atmosphere of the sales ring. If you find a likely purchase, decide what your maximum bid will be, and stick to it. Remember that you are bidding in guineas, not pounds, so if you bid successfully at 1,000 guineas you will actually be paying £1,050.

The ex-racehorse

Reports of bloodstock sales, where racehorses in and out of training traditionally change hands, can make tempting reading for would-be buyers on a limited budget. In theory it is possible to buy a nice Thoroughbred this way for under 1,000 guineas – but it takes a lot of skill, just as much luck and the knowledge and ability to re-school the horse when you get it home. Even then, it may not turn out to have the right temperament for the job you have in mind.

All you have to go on at a bloodstock auction is the catalogue description and your own eyes; you will not be able to ride the horse or ask to see him do any more than trot up in-hand. If a horse is simply too slow to be a successful racehorse, he may well make a successful career change: many event horses start off in training, and there are show hacks who have come down the same route. But if his racing career is curtailed because of a soundness problem, you could simply be buying trouble.

You pays your money and takes your chance. Remember when you bid that you are paying in guineas and check in the catalogue to see if you also have to pay VAT.

A good ex-racehorse can be an excellent buy for someone with the ability and experience to educate him. You have to accept that whilst he will usually – but not always – be good in traffic, he will probably not be used to working alone. Racehorses invariably go to and from the gallops in a string, nose to tail with other horses, and it often takes patient hours of long-reining to get them confident to go out on their own.

Many racehorses are broken and ridden well, but you cannot guarantee this. Some have good mouths whilst others are 'gobby' or one-sided. They usually have no idea of conventional schooling, as they are ridden mainly on straight lines by lightweight riders with very short stirrups.

You have to be prepared to go right back to basics. The only safe way to deal with an ex-racehorse is to assume that he knows nothing and to take nothing for granted.

CASE HISTORY
Spangle, a four-year-old mare, was bought by the author direct from a racing yard. She was in poor condition and had an undistinguished racing record, probably because she lacked any ambition to gallop faster than other horses! Spangle was infected with ringworm when she was purchased and needed treatment plus two months turned out on good spring grass to relax and unwind.

Although she was sensitive, as are most Thoroughbreds, she proved to be a calm and sensible horse. Her good conformation and paces made her an extremely comfortable ride and she was far too ladylike to pull or buck. At first, she was reluctant to ride out alone; like most racehorses, she was used to going out with a string of others. Three weeks of long-reining round the roads gave her the confidence to go forwards and she never looked back.

A year later, Spangle was sold to a rider who wanted a nice natured, good looking horse to hack and show. She has since been successful in riding horse classes.

Problem horses
There is no such thing as a perfect horse, and if there was, he would probably be rather boring. Horses are, after all, as much individuals as people and even when beautifully schooled and well-mannered, have their own habits and foibles.

Problems, as opposed to idiosyncrasies, are another matter. Even though most – and some people would say all – are caused by human beings, they make a big difference to a horse's value. They fall into three categories: problems in the stable, handling problems and riding problems.

To a certain extent, whether or not you take on a horse in this category depends on your attitude to his particular problem. Some people are not bothered by a weaver or a crib biter, whilst others would not have one if you paid them to take it. Again, most of us want a horse who is good in traffic, but some riders would give this a low priority if the horse showed the talent to succeed in their particular sphere.

Problems are fine if you can either put up with them or solve them and the horse has enough going for him to ensure that if for some reason you were unable to keep him, you would be able to find him a satisfactory home. Logic says that if you were prepared to buy him in the first place, someone else will be prepared to do the same. Just remember that it may take longer to sell a horse with an 'if' or 'but' than one who seems to be problem-free.

Stable vices are perhaps the easiest problems to put up with, unless you keep your horses at home and have the sort of personality which gets wound up to breaking point at the sight of a horse cribbing or weaving every time you go out the door! Calling this sort of behaviour a vice is actually unfair; stereotypic behaviour, as leading researchers prefer to call it, is only exhibited by domesticated horses and is a sad sign that we do not keep them as nature intended. Management is looked at in more detail throughout this book; at this stage, you simply need to think about whether you are prepared to take on this sort of horse.

Behavioural problems are a different ballgame, particularly the real nasties such as fear of traffic, rearing and serious napping. These are not something to take on lightly and you must accept that many problems stem from pain. Problem horse specialist Richard Maxwell says that 99 per cent of the horses sent to him – many of whom arrive with the reputation of being dangerous or unrideable – turn out to have physical problems. Even if these are solved, the horse has to learn that something which once caused him pain will no longer do so. Apart from the potential danger involved in working with such horses, it takes time, patience and considerable riding ability.

Handling problems, which can cover everything from horses who like to throw their weight around to those who bite or kick, carry the same health warnings as above. Obviously your riding ability does not matter, but your 'horse sense' does.

CASE HISTORIES:
Tom was a Dutch warmblood cross Thoroughbred stallion with breathtaking paces and jumping ability – and an equally breathtaking ability to rear. His owners, both accomplished show jumpers, were advised by several experts that they should get rid of him or have him put down, but they knew that Tom was basically a kind natured horse and were determined to do the best for him.

Luckily for Tom, they sent him to Richard Maxwell. Max, as he is known, works by understanding the horse's body language and psychology – though in a very practical, down to earth way. He always starts by getting the horse checked for physical problems, and Tom needed treatment in several areas. Even when the problems were solved, his attitude remained the same.

Tom had been turned out with a group of mares for two years and was used to being dominant. He expected this dominance to continue in his relationship with people and soon learned how to use his athleticism and intelligence: if he reared, his riders fell off

Problem horses can be cheap, but few have the expertise and riding ability of rehabilitation specialist Richard Maxwell. This stallion was sent to him as a dangerous rearer.

and were usually reluctant to continue the battle. His rearing was serious stuff – he could and did go vertical and balance all his weight on the toe of one hindfoot.

Max began by working him on the ground, using the 'join-up' procedure to not only make the stallion want to stay with him, but to establish that if anyone was going to be the dominant partner, it was Max rather than Tom. To achieve join-up, the trainer works with the horse in a 50m round pen and uses his body language to send the horse away and then encourage him to approach. Although it establishes a bond and early ground rules for the relationship, join-up alone will not solve problems.

Max then moved on to long-reining Tom and was soon able to ride him in the pen. The stallion did rear, but soon found that Max was hard to dislodge. One of the biggest breakthroughs came on the one occasion that he did manage to unseat him – Tom

The same stallion just a few months later, now successfully show jumping with his owner, David Hughes.

strolled off, convinced that he had won this battle, and Max jumped straight back on him again. The stallion was so surprised he never reared with him again.

Soon Tom was enjoying his ridden work and the challenges Max was able to offer him. He finds jumping easy and not only did he start winning classes from the beginning, he behaved well amongst other horses. His owner, encouraged by Max's success with the horse, took over the ride and Tom is regularly winning his Newcomers classes in affiliated show jumping. He has the talent to go right to the top and Max predicts that he will get there.

Although problem horses are not to be undertaken lightly, there are times when a capable, dedicated amateur can succeed when many others would have dismissed the horse as more trouble than it was worth. In this context, it is important to define 'amateur' as meaning someone who rides for pleasure rather than for a living, but who is confident and competent.

Sarah Turner and her Welsh Cob, Merlin, are a good example of how patience and perseverance can pay off – though Sarah says that there have been times when she has been just as bloody-minded as her horse! She bought him as a three-year-old, and took

It has taken many years of dedication and patience for Sarah Turner to cope with her Welsh Cob, Merlin. Many people would have given up when they realised they had bought a bolter, but Sarah persevered and the two have a strong partnership.

little notice of the seller's throwaway comment that though she would not find a kinder horse, he would occasionally try and take off with her.

The truth was that Merlin would bolt. This was not a case of a horse who took a hold, but one who took off in an uncontrollable, flat out gallop. Sarah is reasonably sure that he had been beaten at some time, because he was terrified of whips, but she also thinks that he likes to take the mickey out of his rider.

By working him in an enclosed area, with the help of two exceptional teachers, Sarah improved his balance and her control. Gradually, they came to an understanding and Sarah learned the fine line between establishing the boundaries she wanted Merlin to work within and pushing him too far.

It was far from easy, and there were times when she felt like giving up. The day came when she realised that she only had two options: to accept and cope with the problem Merlin posed or to sell him. Sarah decided to keep him, because when things went right she got so much pleasure from riding him and also because she knew that she would be bored by a horse who did not pose some sort of challenge.

Seven years on, they have developed a mutual respect. Merlin still takes off on occasion, but Sarah can usually prevent it and in any case makes sure that she does not put herself in a situation where she is in danger. She knows, for instance, that his behaviour is more unpredictable when he is losing his summer coat and growing his winter one, perhaps because he is more sensitive.

There is one other sort of problem horse that may be offered to you cheaply, and that is the animal in poor condition. No one who cares about animals can fail to feel sorry for a thin horse, but no matter how good your intentions, it must be stressed that dealing with the true 'rescue case' is a job for the professionals. If you are worried by a horse's condition, the best thing you can do for it is usually to contact the International League for the Protection of Horses, the Royal Society for the Prevention of Cruelty to Animals or the Blue Cross.

All calls are followed up; the ILPH, for example, will immediately ask one of its trained field officers to see the horse and talk to the owners and if it is a case of neglect or cruelty, the necessary steps will be taken to safeguard the horse. Many horses who have been starved and neglected can be rehabilitated and go on to lead happy and successful lives, but rehabilitation takes a lot of skill – and usually specialist input from vets and farriers. The financial cost of getting a horse back to health can be high.

So, too, can the emotional cost, particularly if things do not work out as you had hoped. If the horse proves to have long-term damage, he may not have a future. If he has been badly treated, he may look on people with suspicion or even aggression; he isn't going to think 'This person is helping me, so I'll be nice to her'. If he has learned to associate people with bad treatment, he is likely to be defensive, or aggressive, for a long time.

Occasionally you may find a horse who is poor but not strictly a cruelty case. If you have the ability to judge what it could be like in good condition, and the picture is a promising one, you may be able to strike a deal in your favour. One word of warning: a thin but quiet horse can sometimes turn into a well-covered and not so quiet one!

CASE HISTORY

Squibs was a Thoroughbred mare who came out of racing in very poor condition. She had signs of old girth galls but seemed quiet when ridden at a walk – she was too weak to do anything else with. After six weeks on spring grass she looked like a different animal, and when her new owner tried to bring her back into work, she also behaved like one! When anyone attempted to get on her, whether via a leg-up or from a mounting block, she either reared or bucked as if auditioning for a rodeo.

A veterinary check-up showed no physical problems apart from the old girth galls, which may well have meant that she associated being ridden with discomfort. A polo player who appreciated her athleticism and had plenty of his own, eventually persuaded her that she was not going to dislodge him, nor was he going to cause her any pain. She went on to become a useful polo pony and enjoyed this life far more than racing.

Taking a horse on loan

Borrowing someone else's horse might seem like an instant way of solving your financial problems – but if that is your sole reason for considering it, think again. If you can't afford to buy a horse, you probably can't afford to keep one. Nor does it lessen your responsibility: if anything, it increases it.

Nevertheless, there are many scenarios where loan arrangements can work well and give immense satisfaction. Perhaps the most satisfying of all is to take a horse on loan from one of the established charities which rehabilitate problem animals, notably the International League for the Protection of Horses and the Blue Cross horse protection scheme, and provide it with the right home, the right job and the right quality of life.

It is all too easy to be carried away by sentiment and see yourself as a sort of equestrian ministering angel. Fortunately the charities concerned are too realistic to allow this and their schemes are based on practical common sense as well as compassion. This is not an easy option: you have to accept that most horses are taken into these schemes because they have problems, either behavioural or physical, which mean that their owners can no longer cope with them.

Some are victims of cruelty and have been starved, neglected and perhaps abused. Others are the victims of ignorance; sadly, too many people buy horses because they fall in love with their looks and find out that they cannot cope with sharp, sensitive temperaments. This starts a downward spiral where the horse is the ultimate loser and many horses end up at these charities as a last chance.

They have strict loan procedures that ensure as far as possible that horses are matched up with the right borrowers. Your first step is to fill in an application form giving details of your experience, where you intend to keep a horse and what sort of animal you have in mind. The premises will then be inspected by a field officer and you will be told whether or not they are considered suitable.

If you make the 'approved list' you will be contacted when a likely horse is ready to go out on loan and invited to try him. If all goes well and you and the assessors think you could form a partnership, you sign an agreement, pay a token fee – usually between £50–£150 – and take the horse on loan. Part of the agreement is that a field officer will make unannounced visits to check the horse, usually three or four times a year.

It sounds a daunting prospect and in many ways, it is. But anyone who cares about animals will realise that there is no other way to ensure the horse's welfare . . . and although everything is done in a businesslike fashion, you will be treated with great friendliness. You do not have to be a brilliant rider, nor is it necessary to compete: the sole aim is that the horse goes to the right environment and the right job. For some, that job may be hacking or even as a companion to another horse, whilst others will need riders who can give them regular work and schooling. Many of these horses become successful competition animals, but obviously they are only matched with suitable riders.

Private loan schemes offer another avenue, though they can be full of potential pitfalls. There are genuine reasons why a horse or pony is offered on loan – for instance, a family may not want to sell a much loved pony who is temporarily out of work, and will want to loan him for a year or two until the next child is old enough to ride him. Alternatively, an older animal may need an easier life and be offered on loan, rather than for sale, because his owners want to safeguard his future.

The most important survival rule with private loan arrangements is to put everything on a businesslike footing, in writing. That applies just as much when you are dealing with friends as with strangers, as verbal arrangements can lead to misunderstandings and misunderstandings can grow into disasters.

Knowing that you will have to give the horse back at the end of a loan period may not prevent you becoming fond of him. There have also been cases of riders taking on unschooled or problem animals and spending a lot of time, effort and money improving them, only for the owner to take them back and sell them for a healthy profit with nothing more than a thank you.

The safest way of making arrangements is to get a solicitor with a special knowledge of equestrian matters to draw up an agreement. It is a sign of the times that the horse world has become increasingly litigation conscious over the past few years; as a result, several companies have specialists who deal with horse-related issues. You may be lucky and find that a local firm has someone who can help, but if not, companies offering this kind of specialist help often advertise in magazines such as *Horse and Hound* and *Your Horse*.

These are some of the essential points you should think about:

- How long is the loan agreement for? The usual system is to agree an initial period of six months or a year, renewable annually if necessary, and to specify the notice that should be given on either side to terminate the agreement.
- The owner will want access rights, but these need to be specified. You must expect the owner to want to visit unannounced and you must also expect him or her to retain the right to take the horse back if you do not comply with the terms of the agreement.
- Where is the horse to be kept and are there special conditions, e.g. he must be bedded on dust extracted bedding rather than straw?
- What is he to be used for and who is to ride him?
- Who is to pay for what – shoeing, vaccination and worming costs, insurance premiums, etc?
- Is the loan agreement intended as a 'trial run', with you being offered the chance to buy the horse if all goes well? If so, agree the final price to start with. You may also want to include a clause stating that if the owner decides to terminate the agreement and sell the horse, you should be given first refusal – again, at an agreed price.

Sharing

When things go right, sharing a horse is an excellent way of getting the benefits of owning a horse and sharing the problems. When it goes wrong, one or both of you will lose out – and worst of all, so may the horse.

The commonest cause of disaster is when two people buy a horse between them. If the arrangement breaks down, either through disagreement or because one partner can no longer continue to keep his or her side of the bargain, you are left with a complicated financial situation. It can also lead to disappointment and ill feelings. If the partner who wants to continue owning the horse cannot afford to buy out the other, the only options are to find a new sharer who can, or to sell the horse and divide the proceeds.

It is much safer if one person owns the horse and the other shares the expenses, riding and, if necessary, work. As with loaning, it is essential to have a written contract and for sharers to be on the same wavelength. It won't work if standards differ, if you take different approaches to schooling or simply can't communicate. For the sake of the horse, you have to work on parallel lines.

If you share the same interests, you have to accept that there might be times when you both want to compete at the same event. Even if this does not happen, there may be potential clashes if partner A wants to go show jumping on the day that partner B wants to do dressage. The only way to survive is through meticulous planning: work out your schedules as far in advance as possible.

CASE HISTORY

Julie and Annette hoped that their different interests would be of benefit to everyone, including Julie's horse, Bomber. Julie had owned the nine-year-old Welsh Cob cross Thoroughbred for five years, but promotion she could not afford to turn down led to longer working hours and she felt that Bomber was not getting the work he needed.

Julie's main interests were cross-country and show jumping and Bomber, a forward going horse who tended to be excitable, was particularly successful at hunter trials. Annette was interested in dressage and both hoped that schooling on the flat, which Julie admits she finds something of a chore, would be of all-round benefit. It also meant that Annette, who was married with a two-year-old daughter, could take him to midweek dressage outings whilst her mother babysat and Julie could compete at weekends when Annette wanted to be with her family.

Unfortunately, things did not work out as planned. Annette became frustrated because she felt that all the work she put into Bomber during the week to get him working calmly was being undone at weekends when he lived up to his name on cross-country courses. She accepted that event riders had to cope with mixing disciplines, but felt that as an amateur rider who was not interested in jumping she was never going to make progress.

The arrangement ended amicably and Annette found another horse to share, this time a mare belonging to someone who only wanted to hack but was happy for another rider to school her. Julie decided against finding another sharer but moved to another livery yard where Bomber could be turned out all day, every day and be put on a horse walker twice a week to help keep him fit.

Chapter 3
A Home for Your Horse

Keeping a horse usually has to be juggled with work and family commitments, whether he is kept at home or on a livery yard. As the majority of owners are not in a position to have a horse outside the back door, choosing the right livery yard and the right care system is one of the keys to survival.

The price factor obviously plays a large part in finding the right livery yard, but you may have to do some lateral thinking. A DIY yard where the weekly rental is £20 can actually turn out to give better value than the one where you only have to pay £10 if you take into consideration things like how far away it is from your home or place of work, how long it takes you to get there and whether you can save on feed, bedding and other costs by joining forces with other owners to buy in bulk.

Does your livery yard offer all-year-round schooling facilities?

It is also important to remember that there is no point in saving money if the end result is that you are unhappy. There are some yards where you find owners with all sorts of interests; at the best one I have ever known, my horse went show jumping whilst his neighbours on either side were dressage and endurance specialists. It was one of those lucky mixes of people that worked: the yard owner was a dressage enthusiast who was open-minded and appreciated that riders in different disciplines can give each other ideas and actually help each other through problems.

When one rider had problems with a horse who spooked and napped on the roads, she took him on training rides with an endurance rider to whom a fifteen-mile hack was all part of the day's work. The spooky horse's behaviour improved enormously as he got fitter and his rider gained a broader focus: instead of concentrating on schooling in the manège, she concentrated on getting the horse going forwards and listening to her. As this was what she wanted in her dressage work, the schooling sessions also improved and horse and rider were both a lot happier.

If you are interested enough to listen to other people's ideas on keeping and riding horses, this kind of set-up can give you new ideas. The yard owner helped me with my horse's flatwork, and as we worked on improving his ability to lengthen and shorten his stride, and taught him the beginnings of canter pirouettes, so he became better able to meet his fences correctly and in balance and to turn quickly in jump-offs.

In return, the owner – who always swore that she was frightened of jumping – found that working over trotting poles and through very small grids of fences encouraged her horse to use his back end more and gave him something different and interesting to do. The funny thing was that we both realised how versatile our horses were: mine did well in riding club dressage tests and hers competed in dressage with jumping classes as well as pure dressage.

Unfortunately, you can also get a situation where you are the odd one out. If you are interested in endurance riding and everyone else on the yard is a dressage fan, you may feel that you are living on different planets. One of the nicest things about keeping your horse with a bunch of like-minded people is that you can encourage each other and commiserate when things go wrong – but if they cannot understand your preoccupation with your horse's heart rate and you cannot appreciate their frustration at not being able to achieve the perfect half-pass, communication is not going to be easy.

If you are looking for a livery yard as a first-time horse owner, or are unhappy at your present one and do not want to make the same mistakes twice, you need to make sure that you ask the right questions. The following checklist has been put together with the help of adult riders with a wide range of interests and parents who have bought ponies for their children.

• Is the yard reasonably easy to get to? This can depend as much on its location as on how far away it is: twenty miles down the motorway can be less time-consuming than a fifteen-mile route which involves negotiating a traffic bottleneck. Make some test journeys at the times you will be travelling there, on weekdays and at weekends.

• Is the hacking reasonable and are there any special problems? Most owners need to ride on the roads – if you are not worried about hacking because you do nothing but school, you probably have a very bored horse – and busy roads and horses do not go together.

• Are you able to turn out your horse every day? Many yards have limited grazing or turn-out facilities in winter, but you must be able to give him that freedom for at least part of every day, even if you ride him.

• Is the grazing well cared for and is the fencing safe? Some yards still offer grazing fenced with barbed wire, which is unacceptable for horses in any circumstances.

• Are the facilities adequate for what you want to do with your horse? If you want to ride on dark winter mornings or evenings, you will need access to a floodlit schooling area or indoor school.

• Is the yard an adults only one, or are there children as well? If you want somewhere nice and peaceful, you might find hordes of children and ponies unbearable – they probably will not think much of you, either, but that is the other side of the coin! If, on the other hand, you are looking for somewhere to keep a family pony, children are much happier when there are others in their age group to ride with.

• Do you like the owner and are you happy with his/her standards? You might think that if you are looking after your own horse, the only standards that matter are yours. However, if other owners are allowed to do things that compromise your horse's safety and comfort, or you are the only one who bothers to sweep the yard, what at first seemed like happy informality can soon be unbearable.

No one enjoys being around a grumpy or over officious yard owner, but a set of basic rules is essential if the yard is to run smoothly and safely.

• What is security like? If there is no one within sight or hearing distance between seven at night and seven the next morning, are thieves going to find easy pickings? Even worse, would anyone know that your horse was suffering from colic before it was too late?

• Can you buy feed and bedding at economic rates, or is there adequate storage if you have to buy in your own? If everyone supplies their own, can you make sure that no one 'borrows' your supplies or inadvertently uses them instead of their own?

• If you own a trailer or horsebox and cannot keep it at home, is there a suitable place to park it? Think about the security aspect: livery yards, especially those where no one lives on the premises, are favourite targets for thieves.

• If this is your child's first pony, or your first experience of looking after a horse, is there someone knowledgeable you can ask for advice? A word of warning: livery yards are full of 'experts', so make sure your advisor is genuinely experienced.

• Does the yard owner give you a written contract stating duties and responsibilities on either side, who does what and the costs involved? If not, it is very easy for misunderstandings to arise.

The other side of the story

Successful livery arrangements depend on co-operation between owner and clients. Livery yard owners have just as many horror stories to tell as horse owners, so to ensure that the partnership stands every chance of success, make certain you are not guilty of any of the following. These experiences are the other side of the coin, provided by the owners of a large establishment with more than thirty liveries and a small, family-run yard catering for four or five outsiders at a time.

- Can you work out a routine that fits in with the general running of the yard? Most yard owners will appreciate that looking after a horse has to fit in with the demands of home and work, but if you cannot fit into a general timescale on feeding and mucking out you may have to make arrangements for someone to help you.
- If you have an arrangement where you do part of the work and pay for extra help, are you consistent? Everyone has emergencies – but owners who regularly ring up half an hour before they are due to arrive and say they have decided not to ride, after all, and could someone bring in and feed Dobbin are not popular.
- Do you pay your bills on time? The worst offenders, apparently, are not those who scrimp and save to pay for their horses' needs, but those who do not have to worry about money!
- If there are duties which are shared between clients, such as sweeping the yard or clearing droppings from the fields, are you prepared to do your fair share or pay someone else to do it for you?
- Good yards have rules for the sake of safety and sanity. Are you prepared to follow them? Obviously it is not your fault if your instructor does not want to wear a hard hat, but if the yard rules stipulate that no one rides without proper headgear, you have to either persuade him or her to follow suit, explain that you cannot let anyone ride your horse who doesn't comply, or find a new teacher.

Survival strategies

One of the best things about keeping your horse on a good livery yard is that you can set up a fail-safe system of looking after him. Even if you are determined to do everything yourself, there are bound to be times when you are ill, have an emergency at work or even want a holiday without a horse in sight.

There are three basic ways of doing this – working livery, part livery, and DIY networking. Working livery arrangements are operated by some riding schools and mean that you and they share the use of the animal. Provided the riding school is well run, the pony is only ridden by suitable riders under the supervision of a good instructor and the conditions of use are clearly set out, it can work well. It means that the pony gets enough exercise and that the costs of keeping him are kept down.

The drawbacks are that eventually, or even right from the beginning, your child may resent the fact that others are riding his or her pony. The only way round this one is to

If you opt for a DIY system, are you prepared to do your share of the less appealing jobs?

explain the whys and wherefores at the start. As you can reckon on ten as being the youngest age at which a child is ready for a pony, unless parents have considerable experience, he or she should be old enough to be talked to in adult terms.

You will almost inevitably find that weekends and school holidays, which are the times when you will want greatest use of the pony, clash with times when the riding school's lessons are in greatest demand. Compromise is essential, with the pony's welfare being paramount.

Working livery is usually less successful for adult owners, mainly because few people are prepared for their horses to be ridden by unknown riders. The big exception is if you are a novice rider and keep your horse at a school which trains its staff towards further qualifications, in which case he may benefit from being ridden under supervision by riders who are at least as good as and probably better than you.

It is important to realise, though, that you cannot put your horse on working livery and assume that this means he is being schooled: he should be ridden correctly, but the instructor supervising his use will be concentrating on the rider rather than the horse. If you want an experienced rider to school him and improve his way of going, you must realistically expect to pay for it.

Part livery means that you do part of the work and the yard staff do the rest. A typical arrangement is where the owner feeds, mucks out and rides the horse in the morning, turns him out and leaves evening feeds and hay ready. At the end of the day, someone else brings him in, checks him over and changes rugs if necessary and gives him his feed.

The only way this system really works is if you have a clearcut definition of who does what. Expecting the yard to do one set of jobs one week and changing the goalposts the next leads to confusion – and the risk that wires get crossed and your poor horse ends up without his feed because each side thought that the other was responsible.

There are three ways of working out the finances for part livery. One is for the yard to charge you a summer rate and a winter rate, taking into account that tasks such as changing winter rugs and hanging up soggy New Zealands to dry out are time-consuming. The second is to make a fixed monthly charge, in which case costs should be averaged out. The third is to itemise every single task with individual charges, which might sound to be the fairest way of doing things but can be complicated and often leads to niggles and nit-picking on both sides.

If you can find the right partner or team, a DIY network is often an efficient and safe way of looking after your horse. It takes a lot of organisation and you may find

Every rider needs an eye on the ground. Can you get regular help from a knowledgeable person?

yourself having to juggle arrangements to cope with occasional crises, but it may mean that your horse gets more individual treatment. Conscientious yard staff will do their best to treat each horse as an individual, but it is a lot easier to get to know two horses that you look after all the time rather than a large number who may not always be your responsibility.

So how do you make the system work? The following suggestions have come from a group of owners from varying backgrounds, all of whom have established successful networks. In some cases, they have learned from previous mistakes!

- Everyone involved must have similar standards. If one is fastidious and the other less so, it leads to resentment and irritation. Likewise, horses must get consistent handling – it is not fair if one person permits behaviour which another will reprimand him for, or he will not know what is acceptable and what is not.
- You must like and be confident in dealing with the other horse(s) as well as your own.
- At the beginning of the arrangement, you need to agree who is going to do what and put it down in writing so that there are no misunderstandings. Obviously you will sometimes need to be flexible – if one person has an emergency, the other must be prepared to jump through hoops to make sure that the horses do not suffer.
- Try and spend time with each other when you look after your horses. Watch how the other person does things: you might be so used to your horse being ticklish when you change his rugs that you forget to mention it.
- If one person has more money than time and the other is in the opposite situation, you could agree a system where, for instance, one pays for enough bedding for both horses in return for help. Be very careful about money changing hands, because if you get into a situation where you could be considered as employer and employee, it could cause problems. It is often a grey area, but these are the ones fraught with danger: if in doubt, get specialist advice.
- Make sure that each partner has written details of the other horse(s)' feeds, rugs and special needs.
- If you start feeling resentful about something – perhaps you seem to be doing more than your fair share of sweeping the yard – talk about it sooner rather than later. Airing grievances straight away is much less explosive than storing them up until you can't keep quiet any longer.

CASE HISTORIES

Julia was thirty-one and working as a marketing manager when she bought her first horse. Sprite, a five-year-old, seven-eighths Thoroughbred, was not a typical first horse – she was sensitive and needed tactful riding and handling. On paper, Julia was well up to coping with her: she had reached the standard where she could jump a three-foot course and ride a Prelim dressage test competently and had ridden a variety of different horses. Her instructor told her that she was quite capable, with help, of schooling a horse and that she should look for something to match her competitive ambitions.

Like many people, Julia underestimated just how much time it takes to look after a horse and how tiring it can be when you have other demanding commitments. She started off on DIY livery and found that she was burning the candle at both ends. If a meeting ran late or she had a problem at work that had to be solved there and then, she was forever worrying if she would get to the yard on time.

The yard owner suggested that she opt for part livery instead, and it seemed to make sense. They arranged that Julia would muck out, ride and groom Sprite first thing in the morning and that the yard staff would turn her out, then bring her in and feed her at the other end of the day. Unfortunately Sprite became edgy and far less relaxed; Julia discovered that sometimes she was not being turned out until the afternoon and suspected that the girls on the yard had such a lot of horses to look after that everything was done in a hurry.

Another owner at the yard, Mary, had more time than Julia, as her children were both at school. Realising how unhappy Julia was, and having seen the conveyor belt approach taken by the yard staff, she suggested that she take over the tasks that Julia could not manage in return for Julia supplying some of her horse's feed and bedding. The arrangement works well and Sprite is much happier now that she only has two people looking after her, both of whom treat her with quiet patience.

Lynn, Lesley, Anna and Lyndsey took a totally different approach to finding a livery yard. They set up their own, just for the four of them, by persuading Lynn's father to build four internal stables inside an existing barn and allow them six acres of grazing on his sheep farm.

The arrangement is that Lynn, who is also a freelance riding instructor, acts as yard manager and is responsible for the overall rent. The others pay her for stabling, grazing, hay and straw and buy their own feed. In general, each looks after her own horse, but if problems arise, one of the others will help out. Lynn's father would like to build more stables to accommodate more liveries, but they have persuaded him not to do this. They feel that one of the reasons their arrangement works so well is that they are a small team whose personalities complement each other.

Martha shared a friend's horse for a year before deciding that she really wanted one who was completely her own responsibility. The experience she gained during that year showed her just what was involved in terms of time, effort and money and she knew that she needed a versatile horse who could live out most of the time and did not have to be ridden every day.

She found the perfect answer in Busby, a 14.2hh Welsh cob. Martha is five foot four and weighs nine stone, but Busby is so substantial and deep through the girth that even a taller, heavier rider would not look out of place on him. As Chapter 2 proved, anything a horse can do, a pony can do as well – and sometimes better!

Saving money and swapping skills

One of the advantages of keeping your horse on a friendly yard is that you can often save money by joining forces with other owners. Buying feed, bedding and wormers for six horses at a time usually works out cheaper than buying for a single animal, as you can negotiate bulk discounts. Likewise, the veterinary surgeon, horse dentist or farrier's travelling charge is much easier on your pocket when divided between a group of owners – and it is usually possible to work things so that shoeing and routine teeth rasping can be made on a block booking.

Perhaps you want to have lessons from a particular dressage or show jumping instructor, but cannot afford what he or she would have to charge an individual. If you can arrange a joint lesson, or provide enough pupils in an afternoon to make it worth the instructor's while, you should get a more affordable rate.

You may also find that you can swap skills amongst yourselves. If one owner is particularly good at clipping, or pulling manes and tails, you could persuade him or her to do your horse or teach you how to do it. The best way of learning any skill like this is to watch an expert do it and then have a go yourself under their supervision.

There may be times when you can borrow equipment to see if it works well on your horse before buying your own. Saddles are a no-go area, because it is important that a saddle is fitted to an individual horse, but bits are a good example. Even 'best' clothes can be shared – research for this book uncovered some very enterprising owners, including two impoverished friends of similar proportions who bought a show jacket between them. The only time they had problems was when a jump-off draw resulted in them riding one after the other, and they had to do a particularly quick change act!

Chapter 4
Home from Home

Everyone who owns a horse dreams of keeping him at home, however impossible that dream might seem. When looked at from the perspective of keeping a horse at livery, it can sometimes seem idyllic – no more rent to pay, no more rules and regulations, no more driving to and from the yard, no more frustration when other owners' ideas do not tally with yours.

However, every coin has two sides. The flipside of this one is that keeping a horse at home can be even more demanding than keeping him at livery. You might not have to pay rental, but you will have to pay to install and maintain facilities. And whilst it is wonderful to know that you can keep a constant eye on your horse's welfare and that you can set your own standards and work out your own routine, there will be times when you will wish you had the support of other owners. All of a sudden, you find out that things which you probably took for granted – well-maintained fencing and stables, fields that are topped and fertilised when necessary – only happen if you (and usually your nearest and dearest) devote time and money to them.

If you are used to having an outdoor school and jumps at your disposal, it comes as a shock to have to make do with the corner of a field or to realise that putting in an outdoor schooling area is going to cost you thousands of pounds. And whilst you might think that you have worked out everything you are going to need, you are almost certainly underestimating things. Little things like wood preservative, weed killer and knapsack sprayers – or proper agricultural machinery if you are talking about more than a couple of acres – soon eat holes in your budget.

If you only have one horse, he is going to need a companion. Even if you opt for a retired pony or donkey, he will still need feeding, bedding, worming, vaccinating and to have his feet trimmed regularly. It is tempting to assume that because you will no longer spend time travelling to and from the yard and money on rental, you will be able to look after two animals just as easily and cheaply. In some situations, that might apply – but do not assume that it will be the case!

These warnings are not meant to put you off the idea of keeping your horse at home, simply to encourage you to be realistic about it. To walk out of your house and see your horse living safely and happily as part of the family is both rewarding and enjoyable, but unless you go into it with your eyes open your dream will soon turn into a nightmare.

What do you need?

How much land you need varies according to how many horses or ponies you plan to keep, the soil type and your horses' lifestyle, but as a rule of thumb guide, you need to think in terms of an acre per horse. Some owners manage with slightly less, usually by fencing their grazing into small areas and alternately grazing and resting them, using an alternative area such as a sand school to give an extra turnout area and/or renting other grazing to give their own land a rest when necessary.

Horses are destructive, wasteful little beasts who will happily graze one area down to nothing whilst letting another – usually the one where they deposit the majority of droppings – grow long and rank. They will charge round when it is wet and cut up your precious grass, so if your grazing is new enough not to be established or the land is soft, be prepared for wear, tear and the need to repair.

If you have enough land to make keeping your horse at home a feasible proposition, then it is vital to settle the question of planning permission before you go any further. Unfortunately, planning is not a subject that can be looked at in terms of black and white; there are several shades of grey, so it is important to get professional advice when necessary. Going ahead and keeping your fingers crossed that the planning authority will not notice is asking for trouble, and there have been several cases where people have been forced to take down stables that they either thought did not require planning permission or hoped that no one would notice.

Although broad planning policy is decided at central government level, it is implemented at local level. Despite protestations to the contrary, different attitudes are shown in different parts of the country and some planning authorities can be almost anti-horse. There have been instances where owners have been refused permission to convert barns to stables even when the appearance of the building would not be changed, or have been told that they cannot put up show jumps in their fields because they are 'unsightly' and constitute a change of use. At present, horses are not classed as agricultural animals: if they were, a lot of horse owners' problems would disappear.

At a basic level, you will automatically need planning permission if you are talking about stables or equestrian buildings for commercial use. It will also usually be required if you are putting up a building or changing the use of an existing one. The exception, which does not seem to have a lot of logic behind it but can make life easier, is that stables which are built 'within the curtilage of a dwelling house' for the owner's recreation and enjoyment, not as part of a business, are exempt.

Defining curtilage areas is one of the famously grey areas, but the starting point is usually that if there is not a fence between your house and the proposed stable site, you qualify. This means that ninety-nine times out of a hundred, you will need planning permission for a field shelter, though there are 'mobile' shelters that can be towed on and off the site by a four-wheel drive vehicle and are claimed by the manufacturers not to need planning permission.

It becomes immediately obvious that if you are buying a house with the intention of building stables and the curtilage specification will not apply, you must have planning permission before completing the transaction. You can apply for planning permission without owning the site, but you have to inform the owner that you are doing so. No matter how attractive the property, do not rely on the current owner's assurances, however well meaning, that you will not have any problems getting planning permission. If you have to make an offer on a property that is being sold without planning consent, only do so subject to a successful application being made.

You stand a better chance of your application being accepted if it is clear, concise and detailed and shows that you have thought about the impact that keeping horses will make on the area and how you will overcome any problems. For instance, how will you deal with muck disposal? If the property is overlooked, explain to your neighbours what you hope to do so that you can hopefully answer any questions and put any worries at rest. You might think that nothing could be nicer than having a horse as a next-door neighbour, but someone who knows nothing about them may be worried about issues such as safety and smells.

At one time, planning authorities were happy to consider applications for

Wooden stables are a sensible, reasonably priced option for most owners who want to keep their horses at home.

permanent, brick-built stables. Most are now much more cautious and some may not consider them at all. The reason is that some authorities have been caught out in the past by people who have been allowed to build stables that a couple of years later have mysteriously turned into living accommodation for people rather than horses.

This means that you will usually have to put up wooden stables – which are, in any case, many owners' only option on the grounds of cost. Most of the good stable manufacturers will supply brochures and plans so that you can give planning authorities an exact idea of what you are hoping to do.

If your proposal is reasonable and properly presented, gaining planning consent will hopefully be straightforward. If your application is refused, you can appeal against the decision – there is a standard procedure for appeals and you should be told how to make one when you get the written confirmation that you have been unsuccessful. At present, you can also appeal if the planning authority has not made its decision eight weeks after your application was made.

Working to a budget

Stables and storage buildings are expensive and it is sensible to get quotes from different companies. Be careful when comparing them, though: what one company counts as standard may be classified as an extra with another, so what seems like a good deal on first impressions may turn out to be more expensive than you thought. To a certain extent, you get what you pay for, but there are ways of keeping costs down without compromising on quality. Things to think about include:

- When you work out what you are going to need, try and take a long-term view. You might only have your daughter's riding pony and his Shetland companion now, but what will happen when she grows out of her pony and wants something bigger? The bigger the horse, the more room he needs.

    Similarly, if there is the slightest chance that you are likely to acquire more horses in the future, you are better off going for extra stabling right at the beginning. Building three loose boxes works out cheaper per unit than building one, and it is not as if it will go to waste. Storage space is always useful.

- Most companies expect you to provide the concrete base on which the stables will stand and will provide diagrams to show you what is needed. It is important to get the correct 'fall' or slope to provide drainage, so unless you are or have an experienced DIY person it can be cheaper, in the long term, to get this done by a good local builder.

- Do not assume that stable manufacturers know all there is to know about correct design, especially with regards to ventilation. Experts at the agricultural advisory service, ADAS, say that a ventilation system should encourage air to enter through inlets above the level of the horse and exit through outlets, allowing secondary air changes at low speed and horse level.

The main inlet is the top half of your stable door, which should never be shut. If you are worried about your horse getting cold, add extra rugs: if you shut the top door, you are forcing him to inhale dust, spores and ammonia fumes. If possible, have a window at the back of your stable; most designs have doors and windows in the same frame.

- Do not despair if you have to convert old buildings rather than build new ones. It is possible to improve ventilation dramatically without running up massive bills – for instance, ADAS runs a consultancy service and will make site visits and recommendations. Paying for a report may be a good investment: see next chapter for suggestions on stable design.
- Do not be hidebound by traditional designs. The 'yarding' system, where several compatible horses are kept together in a large covered yard or three-sided barn, has a lot to recommend it. It provides a more natural lifestyle in that the horses have more room to move about and socialise, though you have to make sure that you can feed them individually. The easiest way of doing this is to have 'logs and ropes' – lead ropes with wooden balls on the end that pass through rings in the wall, so that the horses are restrained but not as restricted as if they were tied up – at points far enough apart to avoid squabbles. The horses can thus be separated whilst they eat their feeds and released when they have finished.

Fencing

Fencing is one of those things that you take for granted until you have to buy it. In an ideal world, every field would be surrounded by thick, well-maintained hedges; unfortunately hedges take five years to grow and it is very difficult to get them to the stage where a determined equine will not find a weak spot and push his way through.

Whilst it is well worth planting hedging as a long-term measure, because it will provide shelter from the wind and rain as well as a barrier, you will need an alternative – or fencing to act as a back-up if your paddock is surrounded by hedges that are not horse-proof. There are several safe choices available, but, as with stabling, there is more to consider than the initial cost if you want to get the best value.

Some forms of fencing will keep horses in but are not suitable if, for instance, you occasionally need to graze sheep on your land to keep it in good condition. Sheep farmers usually have their own portable electric fencing, but this comprises thin wire that is difficult to see and not suitable for horses.

You also need to consider the maintenance factor. Post and rail fencing is excellent for horses in terms of safety, but it only takes one wood chewer or crib biter to weaken whole lengths. You may also have to be prepared to spend time on it: some companies claim that their fencing does not need creosoting, but most do and it is a lengthy job.

All types of fencing have advantages and disadvantages. To help you, here is a guide to the main types, from the traditional to the most high-tech:

Hedging

Hawthorn is probably the most effective, but it takes four or five years to establish a good hedge. It will need to be cut twice a year and you will need to reinforce it with post and rail or electric fencing. However, high, thick hedging gives valuable shelter and is a real bonus if your horses live out all or most of the time. Horses will often prefer to stand in the shelter of a hedge rather than go in a field shelter.

Post and rail

Post and rail is a traditional favourite, though prices vary enormously: current rates average £5 – £9-plus per metre. You get what you pay for – top quality post and rail comes with long-term guarantees against rot and woodworm infestation and some companies advertise their fencing as maintenance-free in that it does not need to be creosoted every year.

Three rail fencing is obviously more expensive than two. Whilst it is perfectly possible to put up your own, the suppliers will have the equipment and experience to get it done quicker and more easily. If time means money, this can be an important consideration.

Unfortunately some horses get great enjoyment from chewing wooden fencing and will lean on it to reach the proverbial grass that is better on the other side or to relieve

Post and rail fencing is a safe, traditional choice.

an itch. The best way of preventing them is to offset electric wire or tape from the top rail, which protects a substantial investment at a relatively small cost.

Electric

Electric fencing is relatively cheap; one leading manufacturer says that to fence a four-acre field will cost less than a quarter of the equivalent amount of post and rail. It is easy to install and has the advantage that if you move, you can take it with you! No horse would ever dream of chewing it – at least, not more than once – and as soon as they know what happens if they touch it, most will stay away from it even when it is not switched on.

The disadvantages are that it never looks quite as smart as more traditional fencing and unless you can run it from a mains supply, the battery needs re-charging regularly. However, for most people the pluses far outweigh the minuses. If you rent someone else's grazing and are not happy about the fencing, putting up your own electric fencing just inside it will keep your horses safe and secure.

Temporary electric fencing is easily portable and is useful for dividing large areas into smaller paddocks that can be alternately grazed and rested. Make sure that your small areas leave enough room for two horses to get away from each other, or for one horse not to run into the fencing on the other side if he is frightened by something. One manufacturer tells a horror story about someone who fenced a 20m square and turned out an inexperienced young horse who took off at the first 'bite' from the fence. He ran into the other side, where he received another shock, and bounced off it from side to side in panic until someone realised what was happening, switched off the current and managed to catch him.

Stud fencing

If you want to keep your horses in, but dogs out, or if you need to graze your field with sheep, stud fencing provides a cost-effective answer. This is a general term for wire fencing designed especially for horses, often with a wooden rail along the top.

Stud fencing is very different from ordinary wire fencing, which should be avoided. Check that any joins are on the outside, so that there are no sharp points on the inside, and that the wire is of sufficient quality. It should be heavy enough to hold its shape, which ordinary mild wire will not do, and the British Standard kitemark gives an assurance of quality.

Some stud fencing has a diamond mesh whilst others have a square configuration. If you go for the square mesh, check that the squares are small enough to prevent a horse putting his foot through at the bottom. The best designs have smaller squares at the bottom than at the top and are not to be confused with sheep wire.

Theoretically, it is possible to install your own stud fencing. However, as you are dealing with high tensile wire, in practice, it usually turns out to be a specialist job.

Stud fencing is low on maintenance and high on safety. It keeps horses in – and dogs out.

Plastic fencing

Plastic fencing is in all fairness a misnomer: it gives the impression of something cheap and faintly tacky, and it is neither. A new generation of high-tech materials, developed mainly for the double glazing industry, has resulted in fencing that manufacturers claim is chewproof, lasts for twenty years or more and only needs wiping down to keep it looking pristine. Unfortunately for most of us, all this comes at a price and you will be looking at costs of at least twice that of post and rail.

This fencing is designed to stay firmly in place for normal use, but for the rails to dislodge if a bolting horse charges into them. One user says he has worked out that in five years time, it will have cost the same as post and rail fencing, and that in ten years it will have paid for itself. If you can afford the initial outlay, it could be worth considering.

Tried and tested

The National Stud at Newmarket, Suffolk, is home to some of the most valuable bloodstock in the world. Chief executive Miles Littlewort is responsible not only for their safety and well-being, but for the upkeep of 550 acres of grazing and fifty miles of fencing.

Hedging provides a windbreak as well as a barrier but usually needs to be combined with post and rail.

High-tech fencing like this plastic post and rail is expensive but according the manufacturers, maintenance-free.

He believes that different types of fencing suit different types of job. He finds that traditional post and rail is always acceptable, but likes stud fencing along the perimeters to keep out dogs. Plastic fencing has been used to divide fields and a wind-break material provided a sheltered paddock for mares and foals. Electric fencing, offset about ten inches, is used to keep the stallions back from their fences – or, more accurately, to stop members of the public getting too close to the stallions!

School time

If you are used to keeping your horse at a livery yard that boasts an outdoor or indoor school, it becomes a bit of a culture shock when you suddenly have horses at home but only the corner of a field to work in. In one sense it can actually be good for you, because it gets you out of the belief that you have to have an enclosed area to work in; after all, when you go to a show you are usually riding on someone else's field with lots of distractions to take your horse's attention. If you can only get him to go nicely in a perfectly level, enclosed space, you do not stand much chance in the real world.

Having said that, schooling in a sea of mud or risking jumping on rock hard ground

Electric fencing like this is simple to put up and can be used to divide your field into areas that can be alternately grazed and rested.

is not fair on your horse and could lead to injury. Unless you can find facilities nearby to borrow or rent, you are bound to want a proper working area. No matter how you do it, you are talking in terms of a big outlay; at current prices, the materials alone for a 40m × 20m sand school work out at £3,500 – £4,500. Even if you are doing the work yourself, you have to add on hire of equipment such as diggers and rollers and the price of the time involved.

For most people, the only feasible option is to have a school professionally installed. The first, and biggest question, is how much it is going to cost: the answer could be anywhere between £7,500 – £12,000. Prices for a purpose-built indoor arena start at about £50,000, unless you happen to have an existing building that can be converted; in this case, you will almost certainly need planning permission for change of use even if the exterior appearance will not be altered.

Do your homework

You will often hear horror stories about schools which turn out to be unsuitable, but doing your homework first should minimise the risks. Problems range from unsuitable drainage, to base materials which come through to the surface. The following guide-lines come from engineering and construction experts:

- Building arenas is a specialist job for people who know about engineering and construction *and also about horses*. Note that the two do not necessarily go together. If you want to try and save money by doing some of the work yourself, you should get specialist advice and carry it out to the exact specification.

  A lot of problems stem from owners who call in the local 'JCB man' to level a site and put a load of sand on top. A contractor needs the experience to work out drainage requirements.

  It may not be as cost efficient as you think to do a partial DIY job. Unless you do not put a value on your time, the sums may not work out as you would like —professionals can buy materials at a better price because they are building all the time.

- Before settling on a contractor, ask around to find out whether owners of local arenas are happy with their schools. Find out who built them, so you know who is recommended and who might be best avoided.

  Try and find people whose schools have been down and in regular use for a couple of years. If they are still happy with them, it is a good recommendation.

  Do they use their schools for jumping, or just for schooling on the flat? Most people want to do a bit of everything, but you may get consistent reports of some surfaces being better for jumping on than others. If people are generous enough to let you watch their schools in use, take advantage of the offer.

- Be realistic in your expectations. Despite what manufacturers say, there is no such thing as an outdoor school which provides perfect going in all weather conditions. Some surfaces, particularly sand, ride deeper and heavier when dry and are at their best when damp. Torrential rain or freezing conditions will almost certainly give days when the school is out of use.

- All schools need maintaining. This means removing droppings and levelling the surface regularly. There are lots of ways of doing this, ranging from hard work with a rake to sophisticated levelling systems that can be towed behind a tractor or four-wheel drive vehicle. Chain harrows, reversed so that the spikes are upwards, can be effective – tow one behind a four-wheel drive vehicle or train your horse or pony to harness!

- You may not have much choice about where to site your school, but there are still things that have to be taken into consideration. The more level your proposed area is to start with, the lower the construction costs will be – building a school on the side of a hill is not recommended.

  Remember that lorries will need access, both in the initial construction stage and later on for topping up. Deliveries of base and surface materials will be cheaper if there is access for lorries carrying 20-tonne loads and more expensive if they have to be brought in 10 tonnes at a time.

  Wherever possible, the arena should be built above ground level to facilitate drainage. When it is built above ground on a level site, you do not usually need drains in the arena – rain water will flow out through the sides of the drainage bed.

  Do you want a quiet workplace, or one that is surrounded by distractions? Some riders automatically go for the first option, but there is a lot to recommend the second. Horses have to cope with distractions at competitions, so it helps if they learn to do the same at home.

If you want floodlights, you will also need electricity. The prevailing wind factor is another thing to think about if you want a comfortable life.

Bases and surfaces

A lot of people worry about what is going on top of their school and dismiss the underneath, but both are important. A clean, free-draining base gives you a good start – carboniferous limestone is reckoned by many construction companies to be the best, but can be expensive in some parts of the country. Clean demolition hardcore and road planings are cheaper, but will not drain as well.

Constructors put a separating layer between base and surface to stop the base coming through and the surface going into the base. If you are going it alone, get expert advice on the most suitable system.

Surfaces fall into three categories. Wood decomposes and eventually becomes unusable and has to be replaced. Sand is the most popular choice and is cost-effective, whilst synthetic surfaces can be used alone or as toppings for sand. Rubber and PVC are the most common synthetics.

'Complete' surfaces are mixtures of sand, PVC, rubber chippings and fibres, coated with emulsion. Check with the manufacturers as to whether coatings will need re-applying, and how often.

Schooling from scratch

If you have done your sums to work out the cost of a school, and they do not add up to your budget – don't give up. Sarah Hallinson, who keeps her Anglo-Arab mare and a pony companion at home, competes successfully in dressage, showing and show jumping at top class riding level, yet only has a corner of her four-acre field to work in. This is her advice to others in the same position:

'I bought Soraya, my Anglo-Arab, as a just backed four-year-old and for the first year, kept her at a livery yard with good facilities. With hindsight, having those facilities for the first year gave a really solid foundation: I'm sure we'd have got to the same stage eventually, but it would have taken longer if I hadn't had a school with a good surface to use.

When you're working with a young horse, it really helps to have an enclosed area with good footing more or less all the time. It wasn't that I wanted to school intensively day after day – I think that's the wrong thing to do with a young horse, they need variety – but it meant that I could take her in there for ten minutes and get her listening before going on a hack. It also meant that I could still school when it was wet or the ground was hard.

Three years ago we bought a house with some land, which meant that I could keep Soraya at home. It was something I'd always wanted to do: I think everyone does. But it did mean I had to do some lateral thinking; hopefully we'll be able to put an outdoor school in one day, but until then I've got dressage markers and enough poles and stands to make a small grid in the corner of the field.

We fenced it off so that I could leave things set up and have a definite working area. I didn't think it was fair to ask Soraya to work in a place that usually meant eating and freedom!

I miss not having the school, but there are ways round it. You can be pretty inventive when you have to: I'm much more careful about transitions when I'm hacking, and when it's safe I practise leg yielding and so on. Quite often I'll ride down the road, pick a landmark like a particular telegraph pole and aim to halt alongside it . . . which isn't much different from halting at a particular letter in the dressage arena.

I make the most of riding club clinics, which give me the chance to have lessons in indoor and outdoor schools at a much cheaper rate than they would be normally, and if I feel either (or both) of us needs a tune-up, I hire the arena at a local riding school. It takes some organising, because they only hire it out on Mondays, which is the school horses' day off, and I have to juggle my days off at work.

I don't think I'd want to start a young horse from scratch without good facilities, though I do know people who've done it. I think it depends on your horse's temperament and how much patience you've got.'

Home alone

When you keep your horse on a livery yard, there is always someone you can call on for help in an emergency. If you get 'flu or suddenly have to work away from home for a few days, there will inevitably be a yard manager or fellow livery owner who will help out. But when you keep your horse at home, the buck starts and finishes with you.

Nine times out of ten, non-horsy members of the family get so used to having your horse around that they overcome any fears of being near large, potentially dangerous animals. The idea of your beloved horse being thought of in these terms might seem ridiculous, but try and approach it from the viewpoint of someone who perhaps has never dealt with anything other than dogs or cats. Even the friendliest pony can step on someone's toe, and an excited horse jogging on the end of a leadrope may seem dangerously close to a wild animal to someone who has never had much to do with him.

For everyone's sake, including the horse's, it is vital that at least one member of your family learns basic handling skills. It does not matter if they have no desire to learn to ride – but you do need to teach them to catch your horse, bring him in, pick out his feet, change his rugs and give him hay. Just as important, they need to learn to do this safely; if someone leads a horse in from the field and wraps the leadrope round a hand, he could be badly injured if the horse spooks at something.

Persuade your volunteer to spend time with you when you carry out routine care and to have a go, under your supervision. Once they are confident, make sure they keep in practice so that handling your horse confidently and safely becomes a matter of habit rather than something they have to think about.

Keep a written record of what your horse's routine should be if you are unable to carry it out for a few days. If necessary, keep it simple; it will not hurt him if, for instance, he is not groomed for a few days or if droppings are picked out and fresh bedding put on top of the old instead of the stable being fully mucked out every day. If he is not being ridden, you would in any case reduce or eliminate hard feed, and ad lib hay with a few sliced carrots in his manger will keep a partly stabled horse happy.

Things to remember include:

- The horse must be checked twice a day if he lives out all the time.
- There must be a constant supply of clean water.
- If your stand-in is worried about any sign of illness or injury, it is better to ring the vet – whose telephone number should already be part of your written record.
- Try and find a reasonably knowledgeable friend who can give advice over the telephone if necessary, even if they cannot come and help immediately.

You may find that your helper will enjoy horse-sitting duties so much that you have a permanent convert. Speaking from personal experience, you will then find that the animal is 'our horse' when he is behaving beautifully – especially when winning rosettes – and 'your horse' when he misbehaves, chews the fence or does one of the many destructive things that horses manage so easily.

If you are used to keeping a horse on a livery yard, where you are bound by someone else's rules, you will enjoy a new sense of freedom. Even though rules are essential for human and equine safety and for the smooth running of a yard, it is usually a pleasantly new ball game to be responsible only to yourself. But once the novelty of your independence wears off, you will realise that being home alone is very much a case of swings and roundabouts.

Most people miss the camaraderie of a livery yard, where there is nearly always someone to cheer you up when you hit problems, help put up jumps or simply keep you company on a hack. If you are suddenly doing everything on your own, you need to make sure that you make the effort not to be isolated. This applies to your horse's well-being as well as yours – if he has been used to living on a busy yard and suddenly finds himself with just one companion, he is going to have to adapt to a new routine.

Do not panic if he seems unsettled at first, but do try and make sure he gets plenty of attention. Some horses take to a new lifestyle quite easily, particularly those who find busy yards overwhelming, but others miss the stimulus. It is rather as if the person who likes to go on holiday in a busy resort with plenty of nightlife finds himself in a remote cottage with no entertainment, and vice versa.

If you think your horse is getting bored, turn him out as much as possible with his companion. When he is stabled, make sure he has plenty of hay: eating is a horse's favourite way of occupying his time. Some horses seem to enjoy having a radio playing quietly, though pick your station and make sure it is not loud enough to annoy your neighbours. Talk stations usually go down better with horses than pop music!

Some horses like 'toys' to play with. These range from specially designed 'horseballs' which they can pick up and throw around to empty rubber feed skips, which can provide the same entertainment value rather more cheaply. A swede or turnip suspended in the stable for him to chew at amuses some horses.

Hopefully he will already be used to working and hacking out alone at least part of the time, as horses that misbehave unless they are ridden in company are a real pain. However, it is equally important to ensure that he still goes out with others, or you may find that he becomes too excited for your comfort when he meets other horses on hacks or goes to competitions.

For your own sake, have a break from looking after him once in a while. In the idyllic early days, the thought of having a holiday away from your horse may not seem attractive – but whilst he is your responsibility, he should not rule your life. Learn from my mistake: when we first started keeping our horses at home it was four years until we had a week away. Those seven days on a Greek island were a salutary reminder that horizons can quickly become very narrow, but it was also nice to come home and get back into the routine.

Taking time away from home takes organisation and effort, but it is worth it. The easiest ways of coping are either to send your horse on holiday to a good livery yard, or to get someone reliable to look after him (and perhaps your house) whilst you are away. If you opt for the livery system, try and arrange that he and his companion share a field and if they are stabled part of the time, that they are housed in adjoining boxes. Turning out two newcomers into an established group of horses for a week or a fortnight could result in them getting kicked, or kicking someone else's horse.

There are people who specialise in working as freelance grooms and who will visit your horses twice a day and look after them according to your requirements. Whilst many of them are conscientious and capable, the downside of this sort of arrangement is that your property will be unattended overnight and for much of the day, with obvious security problems. The only compromise is to arrange for specialist horse care and for a neighbour to keep a general eye on things for you, though there is a risk that whilst an unhorsy neighbour would recognise an intruder, he might not recognise that your horse was developing colic.

Several specialist agencies employ animal sitters who live in clients' homes whilst they are away and look after any livestock. They do not come cheap, but you will be paying for experience, proven trustworthiness and a constant presence whilst you are away.

Handling horses safely

Teaching an inexperienced friend or family member how to handle your horse safely often makes you take a fresh look at how you do things. When you are lucky enough to have a kind, well-behaved horse it is all too easy to become complacent and to take risks without realising it: I have a swollen finger joint as a permanent reminder of the time I forgot to take gloves with me to lunge a horse and decided to do so without. This horse normally lunged like clockwork, but this was the one occasion when something startled him and he took off at the end of the lunge line, pulling it through my hand with painful results.

Friends have similar confessions. One lost a toenail when she wore flimsy sandals to bring in her horse from the field on a hot day; he too was startled and trod on her unprotected feet. Another left her horse loose in the stable, tacked up, for about thirty seconds whilst she fetched her hat – and that half a minute was all the time he needed to roll and break the tree of his saddle.

Accidents occur just as often, if not more frequently, when people are handling horses they know well. Most of us tend to be more cautious with unknown animals, but to take familiar characters for granted. Statistics show that most accidents happen not when horses are being ridden, but when they are being handled from the ground. The chance of something going wrong doubles when you are trying to control an awkward or frightened animal, so do everything possible to minimise risks.

If there is the slightest chance that you and the horse will have a difference of opinion, wear gloves, a hat or skull cap and boots with protective toe caps. Take no notice of anyone who thinks that taking these precautions is a sign of wimpishness: a horse who hates having his belly clipped, for instance, could easily fracture your skull with a cow kick. Remember, too, that the most basic rule is always the simplest – keep your wits about you and do not take anything or any horse for granted.

Chapter 5
A Stable Environment

In recent years we have become much more conscious of the fact that horses have evolved as animals who roam wide areas to find food and water, so stabling them for twenty-two hours out of twenty-four – as is common practice in many racing yards – means imposing a totally unnatural lifestyle on them. Most people would accept that there is nothing wrong in stabling horses for part of the time, but a stable must not become a prison.

Your management regime obviously depends on your horse's type and his work-load, but if you cannot arrange at least four or five hours turnout a day you should find somewhere else to keep him. As long as he has shelter and protection when weather conditions are bad (and this means protection from heat and flies as well as wind and rain) he will usually be happier out than in.

It is sometimes suggested that all this talk about horses having plenty of time at liberty is sentimentality and that horses have traditionally been stabled with no ill effects. What this does not take into account is that most horses today are kept for pleasure and their workload is minuscule compared to the true working horses of years gone by. An average workload of one to one and a half hours per day pales into insignificance beside, say, that of a farm horse fifty years ago who would work in the fields from seven in the morning until four in the afternoon – and often much later at peak times such as harvest.

This might prompt you to wonder if your horse needs a stable at all, particularly if your riding is limited by work or family commitments. The answer is that many horses and ponies do live quite happily without being stabled on a regular basis . . . but they still need shelter and proper care. Youngstock in particular winter out successfully as long as these criteria are met, but most breeders prefer them to spend the nights of their first winter in a stable or in an open-fronted barn, where they can live with others of the same age.

If you want your horse to live out all-year-round, you have to satisfy the following criteria:

- Is his field on well-draining land and is it large enough to prevent it becoming a sea of mud?
- Is natural shelter provided by thick hedging?

- Is there, or can you provide a suitable field shelter? (See next section for specifications.)
- Are you prepared and able to provide sufficient hay and hard feed? Even if he is rugged up, he will use a lot of energy simply keeping warm. That will have to be replaced if he is to stay in good condition. He will need checking and feeding and his rug adjusting at least twice a day and you must also be able to ensure that he does not go short of water in freezing conditions. This usually means taking containers to the field at regular intervals.

  Good doers such as cobs and native ponies only live up to their name when there is sufficient grass of enough quality. The rate of growth slows dramatically during the late autumn and winter months, and even good doers cannot live on fresh air. Whilst you will save on bedding costs, you will usually have to feed more than if your horse was stabled at night.
- Can you afford to equip him with at least two good quality New Zealand rugs . . . and be prepared to buy a third if one gets damaged? You must have at least two so that you always have a spare.
- Are you prepared to tailor his workload to his lifestyle? It is not fair to give a horse who lives out anything other than a minimal bib clip, which may restrict the amount of work he can do. If your horse is reasonably fit to start with, he should maintain some of that fitness in the field – but it is not fair to leave him out all week and expect him to work hard at weekends. As with the stabled horse, he needs to be kept ticking over during the week, either by hacking out, lungeing or going on a horse walker, to cope with extra demands at weekends.
- Even if you can satisfy all these requirements, it is essential to have a stable available for emergencies in case your horse is ill or injured. As most DIY yards charge a rent to encompass a stable and grazing, you probably will not end up saving much money even if your horse lives out all the time.

Stable design

Most owners keep their horses on livery yards or in training barns, where to a certain extent, what you see is what you get. But even then it is possible to improve your horse's environment at relatively small cost; for instance, it is often quite easy to improve airflow in stables. If you are building your own stables, there are even more opportunities to give your horse an ideal home.

The standard size for a stable is usually quoted as 12ft by 12ft, but this should be regarded as the minimum rather than the optimum, particularly with horses over 16 hh. Obviously the larger the box's floor size, the more bedding you will need to put down to start with – but in general, the more room a horse has to move about, the cleaner his bed stays, so a big box can actually give cheaper running costs in the long run.

Geoff Fairfoull, national equine specialist for the agricultural advisory service ADAS, pinpoints four essentials for a healthy environment:

(a)   Generous air movement with freedom from draughts. For the scientifically minded, a draught is defined as an air speed greater than 0.15m per second.
(b)   A dry atmosphere with freedom from condensation.
(c)   A reasonably uniform temperature.
(d)   Dry flooring with good drainage. Obviously this must be coupled with suitable bedding and good management.

Horses are much more tolerant than people of cold temperatures, but they are intolerant of draughts. Ventilation is therefore vital: you need a system which encourages air to enter through inlets above the level of the horse – such as windows and hoppers – and exit through roof vents. If you are putting up stables from scratch, try and have a window in the back wall rather than next to the door; a lot of stables manufacturers are buildings specialists rather than 'horse people' and are simply unaware of the need for effective ventilation, though it should be possible to alter standard specifications to suit.

A horse will be happier in much colder temperatures than would suit his owner. Although it might seem nice and cosy to shut his top door when the weather gets bad, don't! All you will be doing is trapping your horse with harmful ammonia fumes that are a threat to his respiratory system; if you are worried about him getting cold, use a different rug or add an extra one.

This covered yard is at the International League for the Protection of Horses' headquarters in Norfolk.

Stable ventilation can often be improved at surprisingly little cost by altering or adding inlets and outlets. ADAS offers an individual consultancy service – for more details, contact its equine consultant at: ADAS, Oxford Spires Business Park, Kidlington, Oxon OX5 1NZ.

Horses are social animals and compatible animals are much happier if they can see and touch noses with their neighbours. The cheapest way of achieving this is to put kicking boards up to half the height of the adjoining wall rather than all the way up; alternatively, set a full-length grille along the top half of the wall.

If you have the space available and the costs fit in with your budgets, you might want to consider keeping horses in the yarding system (as mentioned in the previous chapter) rather than in conventional stables. This means building a covered crew yard, or a yard with a roof over one end to provide shelter, where compatible animals can live together. The International League for the Protection of Horses uses covered yards for some of the horses at its Norfolk headquarters and finds it works particularly well for youngstock and for horses which weave when kept in conventional stables.

The downside of any shared airspace is that dust, bacteria and infections can spread like wildfire, so you have to look at your individual circumstances and weigh up the pros and cons. The American barn system, where a large building houses internal stables divided by a central walkway, offers many benefits for those looking after the horses but it can be difficult to ensure good ventilation.

Field shelters

Most horses appreciate a field shelter in extreme weather conditions and will use one to escape the flies as much as the cold. Occasionally you will hear an owner complaining that he has gone to the expense of putting up a shelter only to see his horse standing at the side of it rather than inside – but whilst there are some horses who prefer to stay outside as long as possible, it is important to check that it is not the design or site that is causing the problem.

Your shelter should be positioned on the highest part of your land, which in some parts of the country, is easier said than done, and with the back to the prevailing wind. For one horse, it needs to be as large as an ordinary stable and the size should be extended by at least half as much again for every additional horse who will be using it. The front opening must be wide enough to allow at least two horses at once to pass in and out. If it is any smaller, there is a danger that a horse will be trapped inside if squabbles break out.

Designs can range from the purely functional to buildings which are also very attractive. The ultimate must be the shelters on one of Newmarket's leading studs, which combine stone walls and thatched roofs and are designed to provide the right

Field shelters must be sited according to prevailing winds and land drainage.

sort of protection in both summer and winter. However, few horses – or their owners – can expect such provision!

For horses with respiratory problems, living out with a field shelter, good rugs and adequate feed can be the healthiest lifestyle. However, Dr Josh Slater, Cambridge University Veterinary School's expert on respiratory disease, warns that you still have to be careful. If you have straw on the floor and/or hay inside and the horse spends much of his time in bad weather hanging round the shelter, he can face similar problems to the stabled animal.

At the Blue Cross horse protection scheme stables at Burford, Oxon, this problem has been coped with in an ingenious way. The shelters have concrete bases and aprons and rubber matting has been laid on the floor to provide warmth – so horses and ponies who live out all the time for health reasons get the best of both worlds.

As a last resort, you can build a temporary windbreak from large straw bales as long as you can persuade someone with the necessary machinery to put them in place for you. The disadvantage is that they may only last for one season and at the end of this, you may have to remove and dispose of them. This would not be suitable for a horse with a respiratory problem, as he could eat the straw and ingest dust and mould spores.

CASE HISTORY 1

The Martin family has two ponies who lived happily in adjoining stables at a local DIY livery yard. When the family moved house and had enough land to keep the ponies at home, they put up stables and storage buildings on a small yard and surrounded the complex with post and rail fencing.

The ponies are stabled at night in the conventional way, mainly for security and safety reasons, and turned out for most of the day. When grazing needs to be restricted for the sake of their waistlines, they live in the yard with the stable doors fastened back to allow free access to shelter, hay and water. Droppings are picked up regularly from the yard and the Martins find that the ponies are happy to wander in and out at will.

They have had no territorial problems and each pony knows which is his stable. They have not chewed the stables or the fencing, probably because they have a mixture of hay and clean oat straw available ad lib.

CASE HISTORY 2

Top show producer and dealer Lynn Russell finds that a row of stalls, originally part of what is now a converted dairy, keep horses who have to be kept in for a few hours happy and relaxed. She also finds that horses who weave in conventional stables, even with a weaving grille on the door, show no signs of this behaviour when kept in a stall.

Stalls are 'standing room only' accommodation and horses are kept on a 'log and rope'; a lead rope is clipped to the headcollar and has a round block (originally a small log) at the other. The rope runs freely through a ring set in the wall and allows the horse freedom to lie down and get up, but prevents him from trying to turn round. He can see and touch noses with neighbours on either side, which gives security and is undoubtedly why weavers become relaxed enough to stop, and each stall has an open front and a large window at the back.

Lynn makes sure that each horse spends time in the field each day, but finds that the stalls are convenient and that horses settle happily in them. As the occupants can range from ponies to 17.2hh heavyweight show hunters, they have proved their versatility.

Where there's muck . . .

It has recently been reported that a top racing stable has been carrying out trials of a 'horse nappy' designed to save work, time and bedding. Surprisingly, the report did not originate on April 1st, though it has not been greeted with much enthusiasm by the rest of the horse world. It does, however, highlight the fact that the type of bedding used and the way it is managed has an enormous effect on the average owner's time, effort and budget.

At one time, wheat straw was the universal horse bedding, as it had the advantages of being cheap and readily available. It then went out of favour, because we became more aware of the importance of providing a dust-free environment, and dust-extracted wood shavings were hailed as the answer. These were joined by shredded paper, rubber matting, chopped cardboard and dust-extracted chopped straw and hemp.

Several factors will affect your choice, but the most important must be your horse's health. If he has a respiratory problem or dust allergy you obviously have to provide him with an environment that is as free from dust and mould spores as possible. This should, in fact, be the aim of every horse owner – but you cannot look at bedding in isolation.

You also have to consider the efficiency of your stable's ventilation and drainage, the quality of his hay and how much time he spends in the stable. Just as important, you have to look at how the other horses on the yard are kept: keeping your horse on shredded paper and feeding haylage will not remove threats to his respiratory system if the horse next door has a straw bed and is fed dry hay. If you keep your horse on a livery yard, stable management therefore becomes something of a joint effort with other owners: most good yard owners will be aware of the problem and should be able to arrange for horses with similar requirements to be kept together.

In some situations, you may have to compromise on your choice of bedding. For instance, some yards do not like paper or chopped cardboard bedding because it blows all over the place and is difficult to get rid of; it either has to be burned, when this can be done without contravening local bylaws, or removed by a specialist contractor. Hemp rots down quicker than straw but is not suitable for all horses, whilst shavings rot down at a far slower rate than either.

Other considerations are cost, availability and ease of storage. Most distributors allow a cheaper price per unit on larger deliveries, so ordering a hundred bales of shavings at a time will work out cheaper per bale than if you buy in fifty bales. Some livery yards sell bedding direct to clients, whilst others expect you to provide your own. In the latter case, two or three owners can save money by making a joint order. The same applies to feed, wormers and even shoeing and routine veterinary treatments – if a group of owners can synchronise routine shoeing and teeth rasping appointments, they should benefit from shared call-out fees.

A bed is only as efficient as the person mucking it out. A straw bed needs to be mucked out completely each day and many vets will tell you that shavings, paper and other materials should be dealt with in the same way if you are aiming for the ultimate clean air regime. However, the cost would be so prohibitive that few owners could afford to do it: to muck out a shavings bed each day and replace soiled bedding with new would cost £20-plus per week.

It is usually accepted that in most cases, you can give your horse a healthy environment by removing droppings at least daily and taking up the whole bed once or twice a week, depending on how clean your horse is and how much time he spends in his stable. The more often you can skip out (pick up droppings) the cleaner the box will stay and the less bedding you will use.

Unfortunately, a lot of us have been falling into the trap of assuming that dust-extracted bedding automatically means a healthy environment. It does when it is first put down, but by the end of a week there is a damp bottom layer that provides an ideal environment for mould spores. If your stable has good drainage and ventilation, your horse may well be fine, but if he still cannot cope your only resort may be to keep him out as much as possible and use rubber matting in stables and field shelters.

Never take your horse's health for granted. Even if he seems happy and healthy, avoid mucking out when he is in the stable and take him outside and tie him up to groom him. The common practice in racing yards of doing both with the horse tied up in his box makes a mockery of otherwise efficient management.

A new enzyme system has been designed to make deep litter shaving beds into a healthy environment.

The right tools make a big difference to how easily and efficiently you can muck out. An ordinary four-pronged fork is the best basic tool for coping with a straw bed, but for shavings and hemp one of the best aids on the market is a curved fork with a strong but lightweight handle, sold by distributors of the hemp bedding, Aubiose. Most owners find that wearing strong rubber gloves and picking up piles by hand is the easiest and most efficient method, but for those too squeamish to do this it is possible to buy small rake and container sets.

So what do you choose? The following guide is the result of testing bedding materials to compare efficiency, cost and ease of management. Each type was used for six weeks with two horses; one is clean and tidy in his habits whilst the other can leave his clean stable looking as if he has been holding an all-night party.

When comparing bedding prices, check whether the price you are given includes VAT and delivery. It is also worth noting that manufacturers always quote minimum usage rates, so do not base your costings on their figures. For instance, one distributor advised that only four bales of bedding were needed to start a bed, but eight were needed to give sufficient depth. If your horse is not one of those lovely individuals who keeps his stable clean by depositing only in one corner, keep him in the biggest stable you can find and put down a really thick bed to start with. It will save you time and money in the long run.

Mucking out is much easier with the right tools. This is the Aubiose Future Fork, which is lightweight and well balanced.

Wheat straw is still the favourite on many top yards even though a lot of vets say it is a major cause of respiratory problems. The only answer is to use your common sense and look at your horse as an individual: if he seems happy and healthy, with no sign of coughs or nasal discharge, then clean straw could be a viable proposition. The emphasis must be on cleanliness, as using dusty or mouldy straw endangers your health as well as your horse's.

Horsemen with long memories say that modern wheat straw is not as good as that of twenty years ago, as the combines cut it shorter. Barley straw used to be classed as unsuitable, but this was mainly because the straw was left with the ears on and these could scratch a sensitive horse's skin. Oat straw is palatable to most horses, to the extent that many nutritionists suggest feeding it as an alternative to hay if a horse is a good doer, so unless you want your horse to spend all night munching his way through his bed, you would be best advised to choose wheat or barley.

Wheat straw is generally regarded as unsuitable bedding for horses who like to eat it, as it contains a woody, indigestible substance called lignin. But this argument can be a real case of swings and roundabouts – as one highly qualified nutritionist suggested to me, picking at his bed helps keep a stabled horse occupied and may be better in the long run for his health than standing on a theoretically healthier bed weaving or crib biting!

Getting supplies of standard-sized bales may be a problem in some areas, as fewer farmers are prepared to make them. This is not such a problem with hay, as once the bale is in place it is easy to fill haynets from them, but large straw bales – each one equivalent to eight to twelve ordinary ones – are hard to handle.

Cost for starting up a bed in a standard 12ft by 12ft stable: £3.20 – £8, using eight standard bales at 40p – £1 per bale.
Cost per week: £2 – £5 per week, using five bales per week.
Time to muck out: ten to fifteen minutes.
Ease of management: Keeping a straw bed clean involves plenty of lifting and shifting.
Ease of disposal: If you have enough room to build a muck heap and the skill and patience to keep it tidy, well-rotted straw manure is always in demand.
Drawbacks: Straw takes up a lot of storage space and must be kept clean and dry, which means storing it indoors. Stacking it on pallets and fastening a tarpaulin over the top does not give enough protection.

Dust extracted chopped straw is, as the name suggests, wheat straw which has had most of the dust 'vacuumed' out. It is then chopped and baled in plastic wrapping; some varieties are treated with disinfectant, which is supposed to make them less palatable, but some horses have different ideas.

Start-up cost: About £38, using eight bales at £4.75. (Prices vary according to manufacturer.)

Cost per week: £4.75 – £14.25, using one to three bales.

Time to muck out: Ten minutes to half an hour, depending on the system used. Some people pick out droppings and lift the bed once a week, whilst others prefer to do a full clean every day.

Ease of management: Similar to or easier than ordinary straw.

Ease of disposal: No problem. Rots down quicker than ordinary straw.

Drawbacks: Some people complain that this bedding becomes compacted very quickly, but if you put down a thick covering to start with, it should not be a problem.

Wood shavings are available in various qualities and it is important to buy dust-extracted ones packaged specially for horses, not the cheaper, dusty kind meant for poultry. It is worth bearing in mind that one manufacturer's definition of dust-extracted is not necessarily the same as yours and is not the same as dust-free.

Start-up cost: £28.50 – £46, using six to eight bales at £4.75 – £5.75.

Cost per week: £4.75 – £17.25, using one to three bales. On average, budget for one and a half bales per week.

Time to muck out: About ten minutes for the main daily pick-up and twenty minutes to half an hour for the weekly 'big clean.'

Ease of management: Makes an excellent system for the owner who works during the week and has more time to do a big clean at weekends, as long as your mucking-out system does not compromise your horse's respiratory health. Wet shavings are heavy, so if you suffer from back problems you might need help in pushing wheelbarrows when you do the full clean-out.

Ease of disposal: Most livery yards are happy to let owners use shavings and most farmers will allow them to be put on their fields. However, nurseries and some farmers may be reluctant to take shavings manure because it takes a long time to rot down.

Drawbacks: Be aware that dust-extracted is not the same as dust-free and that some companies' extraction systems are more efficient than others. If you have a dirty horse, the cost could be high – but the same applies to other materials. Always buy your shavings from companies who treat and package them for the equestrian market; some timber yards advertise cheap shavings to be collected, but these usually contain dust and occasional foreign bodies such as nails.

Shredded newspaper is a favourite in many racing yards and veterinary practices, as it is completely dust-free. There have been reports of horses who are allergic to the ink on the paper, but these are rare.

Start-up cost: About two-thirds the cost of shavings.

Cost per week: As above.

Time to muck out: Similar to shavings.

Ease of management: When shredded paper becomes wet, it forms a large, soggy lump that is very heavy.

Ease of disposal: One of the hardest types of bedding to get rid of.

Drawbacks: Difficult to dispose of. In the days when newsprint (ink) transferred to the reader's fingers, it also transferred to light-coloured horses and their rugs. This does not seem to happen now.

Hemp is one of the newer forms of bedding and is claimed to be up to four times more absorbent than shavings. It is hard-wearing and easy to manage and store but whilst most samples seem clean and relatively dust-free, tests for this book found that the occasional one was slightly dusty.

Start-up cost: Slightly higher than shavings

Cost per week: About the same or slightly less than shavings. In the long run, the running costs of hemp and shavings work out about the same.

Time to muck out: Similar to shavings.

Ease of management: Similar to shavings, but slightly easier in that it is more absorbent and generates a smaller volume of soiled bedding.

Ease of disposal: Rots down quickly and resulting manure is readily acceptable. If you keep a couple of horses at home and have a medium-sized or large garden, you might even be able to use it all yourself.

Drawbacks: Our horses showed no signs of wanting to eat their hemp beds, though there have been reports from veterinary surgeons of problems with a few who did.

Rubber matting can seem like the eighth wonder of the world, if you have a beautifully designed stable with excellent drainage. It is used with great success at the Blue Cross horse protection scheme's stables at Burford, Oxfordshire, where it has paid for itself in a year in terms of money saved on bedding.

However, if your drainage is not as good as it could be – or your stable floor has insufficient slope or indentations where pools of liquid collect – rubber mats may not be the best bet. With some makes, liquid and sludge collects underneath and though the mats can be lifted and the floor hosed down, some are too heavy for this to be a task you would want to undertake more than twice a year.

Check manufacturers' specifications carefully, as designs vary. For instance, one is based on a two-layer system of tiles placed over a polyethylene grid, whilst others comprise mats with studs on the underside which are laid direct on to a concrete floor. It is worth asking manufacturers if there are any reasonably long-term users of their systems in your area that you could visit.

Most matting systems are designed to be used with a small amount of bedding, usually shavings. Although owners like to see a horse lying down on a deep bed, they seem quite happy to lie down on matting.

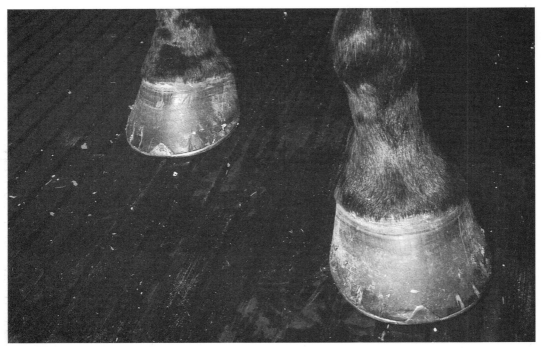

Rubber matting can be a labour-saving choice if your stables have sloping floors and good drainage.

Start-up cost: About £250 – £500 per stable. Some types are still in use after ten years' use.

Cost per week: Depends on how much bedding you put on top. Most users find a thin layer of shavings satisfactory. Some manufacturers advise that special disinfectant is spread over the floor before the matting is laid down and whenever it is taken up and the floor hosed down.

Time to muck out: Five to ten minutes daily. A lot of mats are heavier than manufacturers would like you to assume, so lifting them to clean underneath is hard and not very pleasant work.

Ease of management: On a daily basis, quick and simple.

Ease of disposal: As a minimal amount of bedding is used, you are left with a relatively small amount of manure that can go straight onto the garden.

Drawbacks: Your horse's rugs quickly become filthy, so have to be washed more frequently. One enterprising manufacturer designed a disposable 'overall' which clipped to rugs and could be thrown away after six weeks' use, whilst others make tough, lightweight rugs to be used over ordinary ones.

High-tech helpers

Deep litter bedding, where droppings are removed daily and fresh bedding added until a deep, compacted bed builds up over a long period, is economic in terms of time and

The American barn system makes a comfortable working environment for people, but you need to pay special attention to ventilation.

bedding material. However, it cannot be recommended because the build-up of ammonia and other harmful substances acts as a threat to the horse's respiratory system.

All that could change with a new enzyme system that is used successfully in Italy and other parts of Europe and was introduced to Britain last year (1997). It comprises a powder and spray that 'eat' bacteria, so there is minimal smell, and is used with wood shavings. After using it for six months, I dug out a 'test bed' and found that smell was minimal – certainly less than you normally experience when lifting an ordinary bed that has been down for one week.

The resulting manure can be put straight onto the field or garden and the only problem is that digging out the stable takes three hours' hard work. The cost of the system means that you do not save money, but it certainly saves time.

CASE HISTORIES:
Dressage trainer and rider Cora Roberts has been using rubber mats for five years and says that she benefits as much as her horses. Severe rheumatism means that the lifting and carrying involved with ordinary bedding makes mucking out difficult, but she has found that rubber matting has solved many problems.

She says that if introduced to it correctly, horses readily accept it, and advises that owners who intend to eventually use it without bedding should start by putting a half inch layer on top to encourage them to stale. When the horse is used to it, you can then cut back if you want to.

Shavings or ordinary straw are the best materials to use with mats, though obviously straw is unsuitable for horses with respiratory problems. Chopped straw is apparently not as successful, as it sticks to the mats when wet.

The regime on the Roberts' yard is that mats are scrubbed out once a fortnight. Every three months, they are taken up, the whole box is scrubbed and the manufacturers' disinfectant put down before the mats are replaced.

Nigel Davenport, director of the Blue Cross horse protection scheme, was so impressed by the way rubber matting worked that he uses it at home for his own horses. He suggests that anyone comparing systems should ask the following questions before deciding on a particular make:

- Are the mats likely to move or curl up round the corners, particularly with big horses?
- Is the material abrasive?
- How heavy are individual mats? Most companies say their products are easy to handle, but you may not necessarily agree.
- Is the system guaranteed, and if so, how long for?
- How long has it been on sale and can the manufacturers put you in touch with satisfied customers? It is a bonus if you can see matting in use that has been down for at least a couple of years, but you still need to check that your stable has similar drainage properties.
- Can you hose underneath the mats without lifting them out? How often, on average, should you have to take out the matting completely to wash down the floor?

Chapter 6
Food for Thought

Deciding what and how much to feed their horses sends some owners into total confusion, mainly because there are so many feeds on the market and so much information available. How do you decide whether Brand A is better than Brand B? Is coarse mix better than cubes? Does your horse need micronutrients, electrolytes, probiotics or herbal supplements?

There is one basic answer to all these problems . . . don't panic! As long as you go back to basics and remember how horses have evolved and are prepared to do some basic analysis of your horse's type, workload and lifestyle, you will be able to keep him healthy and happy.

You can also get free advice from feed company nutritionists, as all the big names have helplines. Their advice will obviously incorporate the use of their own products, but should be based on the horses' best interests rather than being presented as a hard sell. Asking the right questions, being persistent and not being afraid to ask for science to be translated into plainer English when necessary should give you the right results.

When we think about feeding, most of us start by focusing our thoughts on hard feed – all those bewildering bags with labels like high energy, non-heating, high fibre and so on. Instead, we need to think about the horse's digestive system and how he has evolved. Ask anyone who knows nothing about horses what they eat and you will get a simple answer: grass. Whilst that oversimplifies things in terms of the modern horse, it is still the best base to start from.

A horse is designed basically to eat. Given the opportunity, he will graze for about sixteen hours out of twenty-four – not because he is greedy, but because that is the way his digestive system should function. He is intended by nature to be a 'trickle feeder', as nutritionists put it, not to exist on the proverbial two or three square meals a day with up to twelve hours between each one. Think about it: if you keep your horse on a livery yard and he gets his last feed when you leave him at 7pm and his next one does not arrive until 7am next day, you are asking a lot.

You will, of course, leave your stabled horse with hay or haylage. That is, or should be, the saving grace of conventional management. Good quality, clean forage is the most important part of any horse's diet and it is important not to fall into the trap of thinking of it merely as a filler or as something to keep him occupied. Having said that, do not underestimate the importance of eating to your horse's mental well-being: one of the main ways to his happiness is definitely through his stomach!

Before you start to think about how much to feed him, make sure that his teeth are in good condition and that you have a correct worming programme; your vet will advise you on the latter. The standard advice is that all horses need their teeth rasping once a year, but many are much better if they are seen every six months by the vet or horse dentist. Twice yearly appointments should be standard for horses up to five years who are changing their teeth; unfortunately we usually start our horses' education at a time when their mouths are going through the greatest period of change, and a good practitioner can help enormously to keep them comfortable and thus minimise resistances.

Whether or not it is possible to feed a horse exactly as nature intended is open to interpretation. For instance, modern grassland is very different from that of even twenty years ago in that there is less established pastureland overall and certainly less that has been put down especially for horses. A lot of people have no choice but to keep their horses on rented grazing that was seeded to satisfy the requirements of dairy cattle and is therefore richer than ideal.

There have also been criticisms from some quarters of the horse world that modern

Plastic dustbins may be cheap – but do not always offer sufficient defence against rats. Metal ones make much safer feed containers.

feeds are unnatural, but if you take that argument right back to the beginning, you have to accept that feeding cereals in the first place is unnatural. Because hard feed has to be stored, feed companies use antioxidants to prevent deterioration. Synthetic vitamins are frequently used, as natural ones are destroyed by heat treatments. There is at least one brand of feed marketed as 'natural', but it is much more expensive than other makes.

You would obviously not want to feed your horse anything that contained animal products; feed companies assure us that there is no danger of BSE affecting horses. Oil from vegetable sources is recommended by many nutritionists as a good form of slow release energy, but a lot of owners feed cod liver oil and have done for many years. As horses did not evolve to eat fish, are those who maintain that feeding cod liver oil is compromising nature right? It can only be one of those issues where each owner follows his or her beliefs and conscience.

Whilst every horse is an individual in terms of temperament, workload, age, type and so on, there are guidelines for sensible feeding. Try and keep the following in mind:

- Feed little and often to mimic the horse's natural way of feeding. If your horse is turned out all day, it is better to feed him morning and evening rather than give him his total allocation in one feed. Dividing his food into three or four portions is even better, but not everyone can arrange to do this. Feeds should be of equal quantity.
- Clean, fresh water should always be available. Empty water containers and re-fill them each day, as water becomes contaminated by ammonia fumes and many horses will not drink unless they are desperately thirsty.
- Horses like routine, so feed at the same times each day.
- Any changes in diet should be made gradually. If you change from one brand to another, do so over several days by adding a little of the new feed and subtracting the same amount of the old.
- Feed by weight, not by volume.
- Store feed and hay in clean, dry conditions and do whatever you can to avoid cont- amination by vermin. Never offer feed that shows signs of contamination, such as droppings, or your horse could become seriously ill.
- Allow an hour between your horse finishing a feed and being ridden. If you have to muck out and ride first thing in the morning and have limited time before you have to leave for work/take the children to school or whatever, there are ways of beating the clock without compromising your horse. See the section on priorities for busy owners in Chapter 7.
- If you cut back on his workload, decrease his feed. If you intend to give him more work, increase the exercise before you increase the feed.

How much?

Ask a group of owners how much they feed their horses and you will get a wide variety of answers, mostly couched in vague terms of scoops, handfuls and slices. A friend who runs residential courses for riders and their horses says she could not believe the differences in perception of what constitutes a correct diet, whilst nutritionists say that most of us grossly overestimate our horses' workloads. It also has to be said that some feed companies are rather generous in their general feeding recommendations, so it is important to look at your horse as an individual and not take the quantity guidelines on the back of feed bags – which are meant to be just that and no more – as commandments.

If you know how much your horse weighs, go to the top of the class. If you are unsure, it is important to find out, because this is a basic requirement for working out his requirements. The most accurate way of finding out bodyweight is to put your horse on a weighbridge; many large veterinary practices have these and at least one feed company has a mobile unit that is taken to large yards and shows.

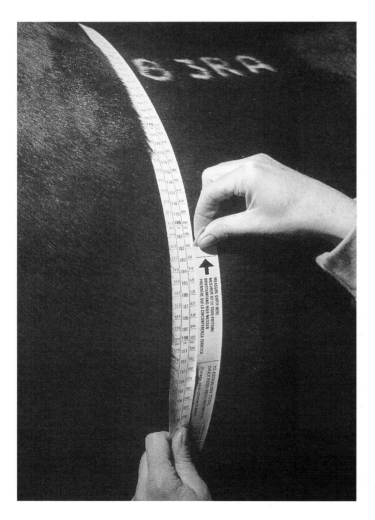

Using a weightape each week allows you to check on whether your horse is maintaining, gaining or losing weight.

If this is not practical, you can use either a weightape or a mathematical formula. Neither are totally accurate, but they are near enough to give an acceptable starting point and provided you always use the same system, can help you gauge weight gain or loss. Weightapes are used to measure the girth and give a corresponding weight in kilogrammes, whilst the commonest way of calculating is to take two measurements in centimetres, one round the girth and the other the length from the point of the horse's shoulder to his buttocks. Square the girth measurement and multiply it by the horse's length, then divide the result by 8717 to obtain his weight in kilogrammes.

You can now work out how much food your horse needs in total each day. If he is in good condition and does not need to either gain or lose weight, work on a total of 2 per cent of his bodyweight. If he is overweight or is such a good doer that he 'lives on fresh air', use 1.5 per cent as your basis. If he is underweight or a poor doer, use 2.5 per cent as your guideline.

Next step is to decide on the appropriate percentages of forage and hard feed. Forage means grass, hay and any chaff or chop type products added to hard feed. To keep your horse's digestive system working properly, it is important that the forage percentage of his diet never falls below 50 per cent. In most cases, it should account for 70 per cent upwards of his total intake and some animals, particularly ponies, will thrive on a total forage diet supplemented with a general purpose vitamin and mineral supplement.

The heavier your horse's workload, the higher will be the percentage of hard feed in his diet – but that 50 per cent maximum applies only to horses in hard work. Hard work means a horse who is in peak fitness for top level eventing, polo or endurance riding; it does not mean an animal who does an hour to an hour and a half's hacking and/or schooling each day with a show at the weekend. The horse who is used mainly for ordinary hacking has a light workload whilst the one whose routine is a mixture of hacking, schooling and weekend competitions usually falls into the light to medium rating.

Once you have worked out the quantities your horse needs, you need to weigh his hay and feed to stay on an accurate track. Obviously you cannot work out exactly how much grass your horse eats, but most nutritionists suggest using a base figure of 10kg for the horse who is turned out during the day. He will actually consume much more in terms of weight, but grass contains a high percentage of water.

Weighing might seem time-consuming, but it will often save you money in the long run . . . and whilst in a perfect world we would weigh every feed and haynet, there are acceptable shortcuts. Some of the big feed companies now make feed scoops designed to contain 1kg of their mixes or cubes when filled to the top or to a marked level; if you use a homemade scoop, you can borrow the idea and mark it accordingly. The most important thing is to feed by weight, not by volume, as a scoop of mix or cubes will weigh much more than a scoop of straight cereals.

Containers like this make it quick and easy to feed by weight rather than by volume.

Filling haynets is not one of life's most stimulating tasks, but filling a week's supply in one go and checking weights with a spring balance, perhaps at the weekend, is quicker than doing one at a time. An even quicker way is to persuade someone else to do it for you: a friend pays her children 10p each to fill the week's haynets whilst she rides and finds that they take it as a matter of pride to get each one filled to the exact level!

Buying and storing hay

You can either buy your hay from the producer straight off the field, as soon as it is baled, or from a feed merchant. The first way is the cheapest – in a good year you will be able to buy in at £2 – £3 per bale depending on whether you can collect it or have to pay for delivery – but you have to be sure of quality, which can be easier said than done. Buying from a reputable feed merchant with a knowledge of what horses require will mean a higher initial outlay, because you are buying from an intermediary, but you should get a guaranteed quality.

The protein value of hay varies according to the age of the grass when it was cut and how well made it is and can range from about 4 to about 8 per cent. This can lead to a swings and roundabouts situation, as younger grass produces a higher feed value, but mature grass dries more quickly – and in unreliable climates, it can be difficult to judge whether or not the weather will stay dry for a long enough period. In the UK, this in turn means that most hay is made later rather than earlier, so the grass is mature and perhaps rather stemmy.

The only accurate way to judge hay quality is to have samples analysed. This is often feasible for big yards buying in large quantities, but more difficult for the one-horse owner. Again, joining forces with other owners can often be the answer, as buying larger quantities should give you greater buying power.

If you find yourself having to rely on your own judgement, make sure you get the chance to inspect a couple of sample bales before buying – and do all you can to make sure that what is delivered corresponds, which means choosing your supplier carefully.

Hay should be stored under cover. A tarpaulin does not offer enough protection.

Unless you are a big spender, you will usually be expected to pay for the bales you check, as they will need to be opened. This is what you hope to find:

- The hay should be dry all the way through the bale and have a pleasant, sweetish smell. Avoid hay which show signs of dampness, as this provides a breeding ground for moulds. By the same token, steer clear of hay which smells fusty.
- It should have a greenish tinge along with that all-important dryness. Hay that is yellow or brown has laid out for too long and/or been turned too often – and the main reason for too frequent turning is that the grass has been rained on between cutting and baling.
- Take sections and shake them out in good light. It would be unrealistic to expect ordinary hay to be totally dust-free, but the amount of dust should be minimal.
- The bales should be dense enough to keep their shape, but not packed so tightly that you can hardly lift one. Remember to judge quantities by weight rather than size.

Good hay will cost good money, so do not waste it through inadequate storage facilities. Ideally, hay should be stored on pallets in a building which keeps out the rain but allows air to circulate. If you keep one or two horses at home, a field shelter makes a good small haystore; you need vents in the roof and perhaps in the back wall, which most suppliers will be able to put in for you if you do not feel able to make adaptations yourself, and a waterproof cover over the front opening. One method which works well is to fix a reasonably heavy waterproof sheet across the front, rather like a shower curtain, with eyelets at each corner that can be slotted over hooks set at the bottom of the entrance frame. A 12ft by 14ft shelter – most suppliers seem to still work in imperial measures – will hold 160–70 ordinary bales, depending on their size.

Dust busting

Many owners feed dry hay to their horses with seemingly no ill effects, which is fair enough as long as your hay is top quality. Others have to or prefer to take measures to combat dust and mould spores, either because their horse has a dust allergy or they prefer to take preventive measures. Soaking hay is the commonest safeguard, but will not turn dusty or mouldy hay into safe forage.

We used to be told to soak hay overnight, but research has led to a re-think. Most nutritionists now advise that soaking hay for anything between ten minutes to an hour, depending on the quantity and how tightly it is packed, is much better. This is because soaking for long periods leeches out some of the nutrients in the hay and means that you end up feeding an expensive filler that is not contributing much in the way of fuel.

It is vital that each haynet or bale is soaked in clean water. If you take out one net and place another in the used water, then in the words of leading nutritionist Teresa Hollands, 'you might as well soak your hay in sewage'. You only have to look at the colour of the water after you have removed the hay to understand what she means!

Hay must be totally submerged if soaking is to be effective.

Wet hay is heavy. To save your back, split your horse's ration into two smaller nets rather than one large one. Alternatively, take a tip from Nigel Davenport, director of the Blue Cross horse protection scheme: he puts dry hay into large plastic log or muck 'baskets' with holes drilled into the bottom, then wedges a hosepipe into the bucket. The bucket quickly fills with water, but when the supply is turned off, it drains out in about fifteen minutes – leaving soaked hay which can be fed from the container.

Your horse will only get the benefits from soaked hay if he eats it whilst it is still wet; as soon as the hay dries out again, the spores will be just as harmful. Some owners opt for steaming hay rather than soaking it: the usual method is to put a haynet in a plastic dustbin, pour over several kettles full of boiling water and replace the lid until the steam has gone.

The logic behind this theory is flawed, as steam is not enough to remove the danger from spores; despite this, some people maintain that their horses cough if fed dry hay but not if their hay is steamed. I asked two vets for their opinion – both said that if a horse coughed on dry hay, it was a sign that his respiratory system was being compromised and that steaming might reduce but would not remove the problem. Their advice was to soak hay or to feed an alternative . . . and each stressed that if a horse shows any sign of dust allergy, he should live out as much as possible.

The alternatives to hay are haylage or hay replacers such as alfalfa-based chop or high fibre cubes. All have their pros and cons, so it is a case of working out the best answer for your particular circumstances.

Haylage, marketed under names such as HorseHage, is grass or lucerne (alfalfa) which is cut and baled when it has wilted to about 55–65 per cent dry matter. This can happen in as little as twenty-four hours, so haylage making is not so dependent on the weather. The bales are compressed and packed in special heat-sealed bags and must be fed within three to five days of the bags being opened.

The advantages of haylage is that the nutrient quality is guaranteed – unlike ordinary hay, in which it gradually decreases – and the dust and spore count is minimal. Most horses love it and it is possible to buy it in various grades: HorseHage, for instance, produces one version suitable for horses in hard work and another aimed at those who need a lower protein level.

One disadvantage of haylage is that it is very expensive, sometimes selling at more than three times the cost of ordinary hay, so that most owners cannot afford to feed it in sufficient quantities to keep their horses occupied. Manufacturers say that using a small mesh haynet means the horse takes longer to eat it, but it still disappears pretty quickly!

If bags are punctured during storage, haylage can become contaminated by moulds and if this happens, it must not be fed. Mould patches are usually green or bluish, whilst white deposits which brush off are usually due to sugar and are not harmful. If you are in any doubt, do not feed it.

There is sometimes a great debate on whether or not big bale silage is safe to feed to horses. As silage is usually made for cattle, by a method which could carry a risk of incorporating bacteria that are sometimes fatal to horses, the answer for most people has to be no. There may be exceptions if the silage is made specifically for horses by a specialist producer and if there are enough horses to ensure that it can be used quickly enough, but never feed silage without specialist advice. If you get it wrong, you could kill your horse.

Over the past few years feed companies have developed some excellent short chop substitutes for hay. Fed on the same weight basis, these usually work out cheaper than haylage but more expensive than hay – but as they have a guaranteed quality, do not need soaking and do not have to be used within a few days of the bag or bale being opened, they have become increasingly popular. Some are based on alfalfa, either alone or mixed with dust-extracted oat straw, but a more recently launched product is grass which has been cut and dried at high temperature.

When working out your overall feeding costs, do not underestimate the feed value in some of these products. Although they are more expensive than hay, their nutrient value is such that you will often be able to reduce the amount of hard feed your horse needs. For instance, Spillers Horse Feeds, which markets the dried grass product ReadiGrass, says that it has a much higher feed value (15 per cent) than hay (average 6 per cent) and that 10kg daily would provide enough nutrients for a 500kg horse in light work.

Research at Edinburgh University is reported to show that horses take longer to eat short chop forage than the equivalent weight of hay and thus helps to reduce the boredom factor. As always, horses are individuals and I have found that these findings apply to some, but not all animals. Horses also have likes and dislikes; for instance, I had one who turned up his nose at anything which included chopped oat straw.

The final way of replacing hay is to feed high fibre cubes, which can also be useful for balancing a haylage which is low in fibre. Their disadvantage is that they are eaten quickly, which is not much use if you are also looking on them as a way to keep your horse occupied. One answer is to feed them via a container designed to make the horse 'work' for his feed (see the problems and answers section).

Hard feed and harder decisions

Whilst many native and native-type ponies (as opposed to finely bred show pony types) and animals in light work can have a diet that consists wholly of forage, most others need a certain amount of hard food. Hard food is an overall term which covers mixes, cubes and cereals and is a way of putting extra fuel in the tank.

The basic decision is whether to use a commercial feed or to feed straight cereals, which means oats or barley. In the United States, maize is regarded as a standard feed; compared to oats and barley, it has low fibre and high oil contents and in the UK is fed infrequently. It is unfair to say that one approach to feeding is better than the other, but commercial feeds are more practical for the average owner because they take out a lot of the guesswork.

If you buy a bag of horse feed one week and an identical one six months later, both will have guaranteed contents and values. If you do the same with two batches of oats, you could be buying feed with different values – the only way to be sure would be to have each batch analysed. The exception is a variety of oats sold under the name of Naked Oats, which has many advantages over conventional ones.

Claimed by the producers to be consistent in quality, Naked Oats lose their husk at harvest and have higher oil levels than ordinary ones. This means that energy is released more slowly, so horses are less likely to 'fizz up' because of the relatively quick energy release of conventional oats.

Commercial feeds have added vitamins and minerals and should supply all your horse needs if fed at a minimum level. If your horse needs less than that minimum level, all you need to do is add a general purpose vitamin and mineral supplement at half the recommended 'dose'. Oats and barley have a poor ratio of calcium to phosphorus, but in both cases this can be compensated for by feeding a commercial 'oat balancer' – confusingly, it will be just as suitable for use with barley.

Whatever feeding method you choose to follow, stick to it: do not mix commercial feeds and straights. Cubes and mixes are balanced feeds; some people add extra oats or barley in the mistaken idea that they are giving their horse more energy, but the reverse is true and they are actually diluting the feed. The only things you can add to commercial feeds are chaff or chop, soaked sugar beet pulp and sliced root vegetables. If you cannot overcome the temptation to fiddle with your horse's feed, give him some sliced apples and carrots mixed in with it!

There is no appreciable difference in values between cubes and the corresponding coarse mix in a particular feed range; most companies give you a choice. To take the cynical approach, coarse mixes are a clever marketing ploy. They look appetising and interesting, rather like muesli, whereas cubes look boring to the human eye: how often have you heard someone say that their horse's coarse mix looks 'good enough to eat'?

In general, this is judging horse feed by human values and your horse will probably not care whether he eats cubes or mix. Some people maintain that with coarse mix, you

Sliced apples and carrots are appreciated by most horses and will often help to tempt a fussy feeder.

can see the separate ingredients – but you cannot judge their quality! There is undoubt-edly a minority of horses which finds coarse mix more tempting, but I have never owned one who turned up his or her nose at cubes. They are usually cheaper than mixes, too.

Do not compare coarse mixes and cubes by volume rather than weight. The bags might look to be the same size, and you might get as many scoops from each, but a scoop of coarse mix will usually weigh less than a scoop of cubes. Many companies sell coarse mixes in 20kg bags and cubes in 25kg bags; the weights are clearly marked, so do not assume that one is the same as the other.

There are so many feed companies that you may well feel spoiled for choice. As well as the big names, there are many reputable, smaller manufacturers who sell on a regional rather than a national basis. The 'big boys' say that they have the buying power to buy top quality ingredients and the money to invest in research, but many owners are just as happy with more local manufacturers.

It all comes down to availability, price and market research. Draw up a list of possi-bles and ring them up. Do they have someone who can give expert advice on how and what you should feed your horse? Is he or she qualified and a hands-on horse person? Science is vital, but so is the appliance of science in the real world: you should not neces-sarily expect a nutritionist to own a horse or even to ride regularly, though many do, but he or she must be in constant contact with those who do and be able to assess real horses as well as statistics.

If you compete at affiliated level, you will need to feed a product that is guaranteed free from prohibited substances, as laid down by organisations such as the British Show Jumping Association. Some of the smaller feed companies are unable to supply this guarantee and there is a risk – admittedly a minute one – that your horse may be subject to a random dope test that shows up a banned substance. Check how and where feeds are made. If feeds are made at a mill which also produces rations for, say, cattle or pigs, is there a risk of cross contamination? Stringent cleaning procedures may remove any risk, but it is worth checking.

The sugar question

One of the most controversial feeding issues of recent time is whether some horses have an intolerance to sugar. Several companies have developed feeds marketed as suitable for those who show signs of sugar intolerance – in other words, behavioural problems – but there are two sides to the story. On one side stand those who say that sugar intolerance is a recognised condition and claim case histories to prove it, whilst on the other are those who regard it as a marketing hype. The middle ground is reserved for those who are not sure and/or prefer to keep an open mind, which is arguably the best position to take!

Nutritionists who believe that sugar intolerance is basically a figment of the imagination say that horses digest sugar easily, as they have evolved to eat grass and other pasture plants. The nutritionist from a leading feed company believes sugar has had a bad press that it doesn't deserve:

> 'This comes from the low sugar and healthy eating trends in certain lines of human foods, and from claims from the holistic fraternity that added sugar is not compatible with the evolved physiology of the horse. But as sugar is digested easily in the small intestine, it is unlikely that much – if any – passes into the large intestine.
>
> It is therefore untrue that bowel function will be impaired. This is only likely if a large dose of sugar is suddenly administered without prior adaptation, as when ponies are turned out for the first time on to lush Spring pasture.'

An independent researcher who does not believe that behavioural problems can be linked to sugar intolerance puts it this way: 'Horses need sugar. The brain relies on glucose. If there is no glucose, there is no energy supply and the horse is dead.'

If your horse has behavioural problems such as spookiness or over-excitability, it is important to look at the overall picture. Is he getting too much energy from his food and not enough work from you? Looking at slow releasing energy sources via feeds that are high in fibre and high in oil may help in combination with turning him out as much as possible and checking that he is getting enough work – with enough variety – to keep him right in his mind.

Another question that has to be answered – though it is often a hard one to face – is whether he is simply too much for you. A horse who is naturally sharp and sensitive will always be that way, just as one who is naturally laid back is unlikely to suddenly become a ball of fire. Nutritionists generally agree that you cannot change a horse's temperament through his feed, but you can exaggerate what is there.

If you have looked at all aspects of your care and management and still think that your horse could benefit from a feed without added sugar, then you have nothing to lose by trying it. Whilst researching this section, I talked to several owners, including experienced professionals. Two – including a well-known showing professional who consistently produces top class show hacks – told me that they had seen horses become much calmer when they removed all forms of molassed feed from their diet.

Molasses in itself is not a 'baddie' and although there are several types of sugar, they cannot be categorised as 'good' or 'bad.' Scientific evidence so far shows no proof that sugar causes horses to misbehave or become hyped up, but there are anecdotal reports of animals who have become more relaxed when their owners have switched them to low sugar feeds and unmolassed sugar beet. By doing that, of course, they have lowered the overall energy level of the feed – so if it works, choose whatever explanation you wish!

Supplementary benefits

The feed market is stuffed with supplements, ranging from products with high-tech names and impressive looking research data behind them to 'natural' herbal ones. Whilst some are undoubtedly valuable, others are perhaps triumphs of marketing rather than anything else.

One of my favourite nutritionists says that she spends a lot of time trying to convince people that there is no supplement that will make a horse gallop faster, jump higher or Piaffe better. Human nature means that if we read that top show jumper Superdobbin's rider adds Supplement A to his feed, we cannot help wondering if Supplement A would help our riding club horse jump a three-foot course instead of a two foot nine one. The fact that the said top show jumper is perhaps being sponsored or helped by the manufacturer of the said supplement is beside the point!

In general, most horses fed commercial feeds should get their full complement of nutrients as long as they are getting the minimum specified amount each day; check the manufacturers' information for details. It is usually about 3kg, which will be more than many actually need. If you feed less than the minimum daily amount, add a general purpose vitamin and mineral supplement at half the recommended 'dosage.'

Herbal supplements are usually fed to try and resolve specific problems, such as over-excitability or stiffness due to problems such as arthritis. There are several important issues to take into account here – for a start, do not feed a herbal supplement to try and help a problem without first attempting to find the cause, whether it be something that needs veterinary advice or a communication breakdown between horse and rider.

It is also important not to fall into the trap of thinking that 'herbal' or 'natural' automatically means safe. As one vet with a wide knowledge of herbs and homeopathy points out, curare is a natural substance but is also a lethal poison. Some herbs can be extremely powerful and should not, for instance, be fed to pregnant mares.

Inevitably, our enthusiasm for all things herbal has been taken up by feed companies and others in a big way. There are some specialists who can undoubtedly help when you are trying to solve a problem; for instance, Hilary Page Self, founder of Hilton Herbs, provided herbal mixes which definitely helped two of my horses. But whilst dried herbs might make your horse's feed smell pleasant to you, it is hard to say whether or not he benefits from their inclusion.

Likewise, it is a nice idea to grow herbs in your pasture, but you cannot guarantee that your horse will eat them. A friend with a potentially top class show hack whose nerves unfortunately got the better of him on bigger occasions decided to plant camomile, reputed to induce calmness, and was delighted when it thrived. Unfortunately, her horse would not touch it!

Many owners whose horses are on continual low doses of medication, notably bute, are worried about long-term side effects. There are products now available said to ease inflammation and promote healing; bute is anti-inflammatory but does not have a repairing action. They are not cheap and some vets are more receptive to them than others, but I know of several horses who have made definite improvements on them. One company in particular, Natural Animal Feeds, has done a lot of research and utilises MSM (methyl sulphynol methane).

One major advantage is that these supplements do not contain banned substances, and as horses are no longer allowed to compete in affiliated competitions whilst on bute, they can be the answer.

Problem solving

Problem: My horse is a fussy eater/poor doer.

Solution: If your horse is normally a healthy eater and suddenly goes off his food, check his temperature, respiration and general well-being. If these give cause for concern, get veterinary advice immediately. Get your vet or horse dentist to make sure that his teeth are in good condition.

If he is leaving food in his manger or not clearing it all at once, you may be overloading him. Alternatively, he may prefer to eat in peace and quiet and is not being given the chance. A few horses are too bothered about what is going on around them to eat and tend to grab a mouthful of food, rush to the door, go back for another mouthful and so on. They often settle if their food is put in a manger which hooks on to their stable door, so they can eat and watch at the same time.

Does your horse's neighbour eat from a manger mounted in the adjoining corner? Some horses are disturbed by this even when there are dividing walls between the two, but eat happily when the mangers are as far apart as possible.

Just as some people tend towards plumpness and others stay slim, so some horses are more inclined than others to put on weight. Your horse should be in good condition for his type: he should not be so fat that you cannot feel his ribs, nor should he be so thin that you can see them clearly. A horse with a large percentage of cold blood will usually be more inclined to put on weight than a Thoroughbred or one with a large percentage of Thoroughbred blood, so do not try and turn him into something he is not.

If he is a genuinely 'picky' feeder, adding sliced apples or carrots may tempt him, as may offering his feed dampened rather than dry. Keep mangers and feed buckets clean, as some horses are particularly fastidious.

Problem: My horse eats his hard feed and hay too quickly.

Solution: If he is stabled for longish periods and you want to stop him becoming bored, mix chaff or chop with his hard feed. There is also a special feed container designed to make him 'work' for his food: hard feed goes in the centre of a small barrel with holes that release a small amount at a time, so the horse has to push it around to get the food out.

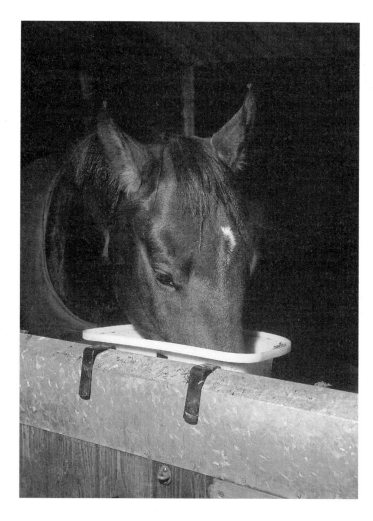

Horses who like to keep an eye on what is going on may prefer to eat from a door manger.

Hay may last longer if you feed it in a small mesh net. As an alternative to buying one, try filling an ordinary haynet and putting it inside another.

Problem: My horse is fizzy/lazy.
Solution: Nutritionists often get calls from owners who want to change their horses' temperaments through feeding. This is impossible, but there are ways of working with rather than against nature.

The fizzy horse is best suited by feeds that release energy slowly, such as soaked sugar beet pulp, dried grass and alfalfa based products and commercial feeds with a high level of digestible fibre. Problems are often exaggerated when horses are given feeds containing a high level of cereals, which release energy quickly – so the effect kicks in about an hour after he has eaten, which is often just when he is ridden.

Turn your horse out as much as possible and when you have eliminated all other causes of behavioural 'problems', perhaps try a herbal mix formulated by a specialist company to promote calmness. These usually either have the effect you hoped for or none at all. Cynics maintain that they work because the rider expects them to and therefore rides in a calmer, more relaxed way – but as long as they work, who cares?

The horse who takes a laid-back approach to life represents the opposite side of the coin. Make sure that he is fit as opposed to fat and that his general health is good: there is a big difference between laziness and listlessness. Is his present diet balanced – if you are restricting the amount he gets to eat because of a tendency to put on weight, is he getting the right basic nutrients via a general vitamin and mineral supplement or a good feed balancer?

Is he bored or could part of the problem be lack of schooling? Most young horses have to learn to go forwards, and many cob and heavier types are so good natured that people take them too much for granted. Has he become 'desensitised' by a rider who continually kicks or nags with his or her legs?

If you get the right answers to all these questions, contact your feed company nutritionist for advice on feeding small amounts of feeds which release energy quickly, such as cereal-based ones. Do not be tempted to simply pump him full of oats or racehorse cubes because you could end up with more problems than you started with.

Problem: One friend says I should feed my horse a bran mash every week whilst another says this is bad management. Who is right?
Solution: Giving a weekly bran mash before a horse's day off work is an old tradition that modern nutritionists would like to see disappear altogether. It is the equivalent of giving your horse a laxative once a week – and why would you want to do that? Bran mashes should only be fed for specific purposes, on veterinary advice.

If your horse has a day off, then cut out hard feed. By all means give him a small amount of chop or chaff with sliced apples and carrots to keep to his feeding routine, but unless he is difficult to keep weight on or he lives out all the time and needs his food to help him keep warm, stick to forage. The horse who is on enforced box rest, perhaps because of injury, may present a different problem. Most feed companies formulate feeds that are suitable for this regime, so ask their nutritionists for advice.

Problem: My horse won't drink when we are away from home.
Solution: If you are away just for the day, take water from home. If you are away for longer, do the same and mix a small amount of the 'new' water in with the home supply, gradually altering the balance.

Endurance riders have some interesting ways of coping with this problem, as their horses have to be persuaded to drink on long rides. One method is to mix a small amount of peppermint cordial in with the water and another is to offer the horse water in which sugar beet has been soaked. One top rider says that the only way she can persuade her horse is to remove his bit and rinse the bit in a bucket of clean water. Her horse then accepts the taste as being familiar and is happy to drink.

If you are worried that your horse is not drinking enough at home, try a tip from researchers at the Animal Health Trust, Newmarket. Their work into acclimatising horses for the heat and humidity of the Atlanta Olympics showed that some horses are happier to drink from wall-mounted containers than from ones placed on the ground. Their reasoning is that a horse who puts his head to the ground feels more vulnerable as he is less likely to spot approaching aggressors – remember that the domesticated horse still has the instincts of a prey animal.

The horse who takes delight in kicking over his water bucket can often be foiled by placing it inside a large tyre. Alternatively, use a wall-mounted container.

Chapter 7
Keeping up Appearances

Trying to keep your horse looking smart when you only have an hour before work and he has rolled in the mud, or spent the night transferring as much of his bed as possible from the floor to his mane and tail, may sometimes seem impossible. Compare him with the immaculately turned out horses in magazine photographs and you may even wonder if they belong to the same species. But whilst it is natural to want your horse to look smart – and keeping his coat healthy is part of good management – you have to work out your priorities.

Basic grooming enables you to handle your horse, assess his state of mind and notice any danger signs such as heat in a limb, a shoe with a risen clench, a foreign body stuck in a hoof or the start of mud fever. It also enables you to make sure that there is no dried mud on areas where tack or rugs will rest and where rubbing could set up a skin infection. But if you are working against the clock, you may find that you have to stick to the basics and leave finishing touches for days when you have time to spare. It does not really matter if he has shavings in his tail or his mane needs pulling; you might notice details like this, but your horse certainly won't. When every minute is important, make the most of your riding time.

One way of doing this is to make sure that you are organised. Some people find this easier than others: as one of 'the others', I sympathise with anyone who feels that he or she spends a lot of time running round in circles. Office manager Jane Welch, who owns a Welsh Cob cross Thoroughbred mare with whom she competes at riding club level, is one of those people who never seems to be in a hurry but always gets things done. These are some of her suggestions for establishing a routine:

- Do as much as you can the night before. You can give your horse a thorough groom in the dark, but you cannot ride. This means that all you have to do is check him, pick out his feet and give him a quick brush over before your morning ride.
- Leave everything you will need next morning in one place, if possible. If you keep your tack at the yard, leave your hat, schooling whip and grooming kit next to it. You can waste a lot of time walking backwards and forwards because you forgot something.
- If you arrive in the dark and muck out before you ride, tie your horse up outside with a small haynet whilst you see to his box. If other horses on the yard are fed

at a time which would not allow him to digest a full feed before you ride, give him a token handful of chaff and two or three sliced carrots. This will not cause digestive problems, but will mean you are not facing a (justifiably) unhappy or stroppy horse who does not appreciate the fact that other horses are being fed but he is not.

- When time is strictly limited, save serious schooling for another day. It is better to hack out and both arrive back in a relaxed frame of mind than to hit a problem and either force the issue because time is running out, or give up.
- The more spare girths and numnahs you can afford, the better! This means you always have clean, dry ones ready to put on and unless your tack gets muddy or wet you can get by with simply rinsing the bit every time you ride. We all know that in theory, we should take our tack to pieces and clean it every time it is used, but in real life a thorough clean once or twice a week is acceptable.
- If your horse is an enthusiastic roller, a good quality neck cover attached to his New Zealand rug means you do not have to spend hours getting mud out of his mane. Some people use stretch hoods with holes for eyes and ears that cover most of the horse's face, but if these slip and cover the eyes, the horse could panic.

Appearance versus welfare

Some breeds and types are traditionally turned out in particular ways, so you have to decide whether you are going to stick faithfully to breed society protocols or adapt them if doing so would make life easier. For instance, Exmoor ponies are supposed to be shown exactly as nature intended, with not so much as an inch trimmed from the bottom of their tails – but if this leads to balls of mud or snow gathering at the bottom, would you be better off keeping your Exmoor's tail at a more practical length?

There are also controversial issues where tradition or fashion and welfare are thought by some owners to clash. The obvious dilemma is whether you trim off your horse's whiskers to give the clean lines demanded by the showing world, or leave them on to act as 'feelers'. Most horses do not seem worried if their whiskers are trimmed, but this year I came across one who was deeply disturbed by it. For the next couple of days he did not want anyone to touch his nose and jumped when he touched his muzzle against anything. In his case, the only kind thing to do was to let his whiskers grow again and leave them in place.

Some people take the issue farther and do not like to pull their horses' manes or tails. They reason that some horses object to having hairs pulled out and that horses grow tail hair for protection against weather and insects. If you want to shorten and thin a mane without pulling, there are ways of getting a neat appearance – see the section on alternative strategies in the next section.

There are also two points of view on whether or not heel feathers should be trimmed. Some say that long hair round the heels and fetlocks helps prevent mud fever, whilst others believe that the opposite is true. Logic would say that long leg hair that is wet

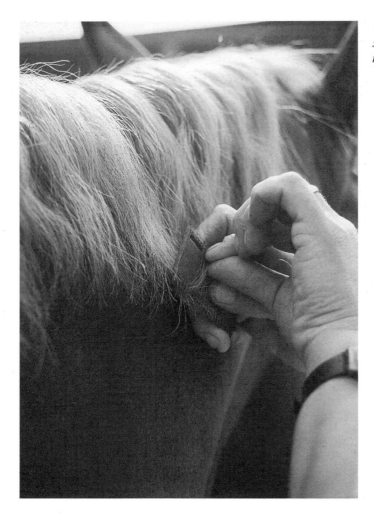

Use an old clipper blade to shorten rather than thin a mane.

and dirty for long periods would provide a good breeding ground for bacteria and skin infections, and heavy horses with plentiful feather are prone to an irritating condition called greasy heel.

The professional touch

When you do want your horse to look extra smart for a special occasion, such as a show or competition, borrow some tips from the showing world even if showing itself is something you are not particularly interested in. Whilst a dressage judge, for instance, will not allow extra marks for the quality of your plaits, he or she is bound to form a good initial impression if you and your horse are immaculately turned out.

Professionals say that to make the most of your horse – in other words, to draw

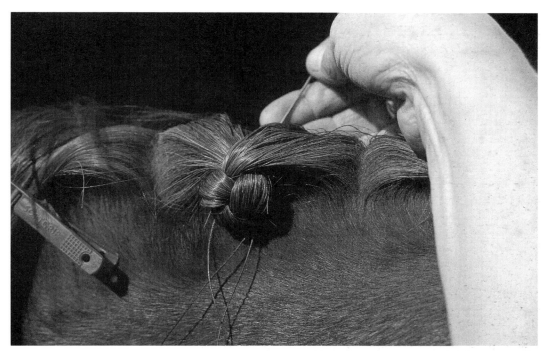

Plaiting a mane to professional standards is a mixture of practice and technique.

attention to his good points and minimise any not so good ones – you have to pay attention to detail. You also have to decide how much strimming and trimming is fair to your horse's lifestyle and how much time you want to devote to keeping him looking smart.

For instance, a nicely pulled tail looks smart, but needs frequent attention to keep it that way. If you do not have the time or inclination to put a tail bandage on your horse three times a week, you might be better off leaving his tail full and plaiting it for competitions.

Showing yards and other competition yards bath their horses all-year-round as a matter of course, seemingly without ill effects. Showing professional Lynn Russell says that as long as you are considerate, your horse should not come to any harm. Her brand of consideration and common sense means:

- Pick the right day: do not try and bath your horse when it is cold, wet and windy.
- Be organised. Get everything you are going to need ready before you start, including suitable rugs to put on a wet horse. Thermal knitted rugs such as those made by Thermatex and Lansdown transfer moisture from the horse's coat to the outside of the fabric, keeping him warm and drying him off at the same time.

Light-coloured horses – greys, palominos, piebalds and skewbalds – can be a nightmare to keep clean in winter. Rugs with neck covers help, and you can now buy 'rinseless' shampoos to get rid of stable stains. These are formulated so that you can apply them to the coat, leave to dry and then brush out . . . when hopefully the dirt will disappear at the same time.

The right lengths

The traditional way of shortening and thinning manes is to pull them, removing a few hairs at a time from underneath. A lot of horses do not object to this at all, as long as it is done with common sense and consideration.

The best time to pull a mane is when your horse has been worked, because when he is warm the hairs will come out more easily. Pull just a few at a time and if your horse objects, try pulling in an upwards rather than a downwards direction. If you want to plait your horse, aim to end up with an even thickness and a mane that is four to five inches long. Some people like to pull them even shorter, but this only works if you do not want to plait – and may encourage the hair to stand up rather than lie flat.

With a thick mane, pulling will thin and shorten it at the same time. If your horse has a naturally fine mane, as is the case with many Thoroughbreds, you may want to shorten it without losing any thickness. In this case, comb the mane through, then backcomb the top layer and use an old clipper blade to shorten the hair underneath, working on a small section at a time. This gives a natural looking line rather than the obviously cut look you would get with scissors. You can also buy a special tool incorporating a comb and blade, but it is relatively expensive and the blade cannot be removed and re-sharpened.

There are two ways of working; one is to finish a small area at a time and the other is to work along the length of the mane, a little at a time. The advantage of the latter method is that if you want to pull the mane over several days – which will often persuade a restless horse to stand still – your horse does not look as if he has had an accident with a lawn mower whilst your tidying up campaign is in progress.

If you want to trim the hair at the withers and under the bridle, take off as little as possible. Try and keep the latter to no more than the width of the bridle headpiece, or you end up with ugly gaps. If your horse has a sparse forelock and you want to plait, you may find that you are better off not trimming this area at all so that you can 'borrow' a section of hair to bulk out the plait.

Pulling tails is more difficult and obviously means you are working at the potentially dangerous end. Some horses object whilst others accept it with no fuss; again, it is only fair to work in short bursts whilst the horse is warm and to remove only a few hairs at a time. You may be advised to pull your horse's tail over the stable door, but this is a risky way of doing it – if the horse kicks, he is likely to kick out the door and damage you at the same time. A safer way is to get someone to hold him and build a straw bale barrier behind him, so that if he kicks out his hoof connects with the bales rather than you.

Your safety must always be the main priority. If your horse is really difficult, it is not worth the risk or the bother. A neatly plaited tail is certainly suitable for dressage and is becoming more so in the show ring. Certainly it is becoming a more common sight and at a recent showing masterclass organised to find potential show horses, leading showman and judge Robert Oliver said he found a plaited tail perfectly acceptable.

One thing that definitely makes a difference to a horse's appearance is a tail cut straight across (banged) at the appropriate length for his type. In most cases, this means shortening it to the level whereby it falls to between two and four inches below the point of the hock when the horse is on the move. Get someone to put a hand under the horse's dock to mimic his natural tail carriage, as it is always slightly higher than when he is standing still.

Perfect plaits

Plaiting a mane is one of those skills which seems easy enough in theory – but getting the perfect results is much more difficult. Professionals use simple but clever techniques that avoid drawbacks such as uneven plaits and wispy necklines, but practice still makes perfect. Show producer Lynn Russell can create a perfectly plaited mane in twenty minutes, but do not be surprised if your early attempts take you an hour or even longer.

You can only make a neat row of symmetrical plaits if your horse's mane is the same length and thickness throughout, so it will probably need to be shortened and/or thinned using one of the methods outlined earlier. If your horse is a breed or type who is traditionally exhibited with a natural mane, you may still find that there are occasions when you want to keep the long hair out of the way; in this case, see the next section on special plaits.

The mane needs to be clean so that when the plaits are in place, you do not get flakes of grease spoiling the appearance. A dirty plaited mane looks as if the horse has a bad case of dandruff! Unfortunately, a newly washed mane is more difficult to plait, because clean hair is slippery, so to get the best of both worlds you need to shampoo it a couple of days before you want to plait.

Decide how many plaits would suit your horse. The traditional number was seven or nine along the neck plus one for the forelock, but these days no one bothers to count. If the horse is slightly short in the neck, then a greater number of plaits – within reason – helps to give the illusion of slightly more length. To get the best results, stitch them in place: you can fasten plaits with rubber bands, but they will not be as secure or look as smart.

Work out through trial and error what suits your horse, then divide the mane into

A running plait is a practical and attractive way of keeping a long mane out of the way. It is a technique often used on breeds such as Welsh Cobs and Arabs, who traditionally have unpulled manes and tails.

equal sections. An easy way of doing this is to cut an ordinary plastic comb so that it is the width of one section; all you then need to do is to comb down the mane and separate a section at a time as you plait. A plastic hair clip can be used to keep the rest of the mane out of the way.

Dampen each section before you start plaiting. You will always find that there are short hairs at the top of the mane, but spraying them with hair gel – the sort designed for humans rather than horses – helps keep them in place. Do not be tempted to pull them out, or they will stick up in a row of little spikes as replacement hairs grow.

Keep each plait tight from the base as you plait down and plait as close to the end as you can. Weave in the thread for the last inch, pass the needle from the back of the plait to the front and secure the end. Now turn under the end and wrap the thread round it to keep the loose hairs together.

Push the needle through the underneath at the base so that the plait doubles back to the neck, then roll up the plait to the neck and fasten with a couple of stitches. If your horse has a slightly weak neck and you want to give the impression of extra topline, push back on the plaits as you stitch so that they sit right on top of the neck.

Forelocks often have lots of wispy hairs at the side which are difficult to take into an ordinary plait. If you have nimble fingers, you can use the same technique as for plaiting tails to achieve a neater result.

Plaiting in itself does not damage the hair, but you need to be careful when taking the plaits out. Use a dressmaker's stitch unpicker to break through the thread rather than cutting it with scissors, when it is all too easy to cut the mane hair by mistake.

Alternative plaits

If you own a native pony or pure-bred Arab and follow the tradition that their manes should be left natural, you may still find that there are occasions when flying hair gets in the way. The answer is to put a full mane into a running or Spanish plait.

For a running plait, take a section of mane near the ears as if you were going to make an ordinary plait. As you plait down, take in a small piece of mane every time you pass the left hand section over the centre one. Let the mane fall naturally rather than pulling it tight and you will find that it will curve round as you continue plaiting until you end up with one long plait along the bottom edge of the mane. When there is no more hair to take in, fasten the ends as for an ordinary plait.

A Spanish plait is made with the same technique, but runs tight to the crest of the neck. Use exactly the same methods, but keep the plait pulled tight as you go.

Plaiting a tail

Many people believe that a beautifully plaited tail looks far nicer than a pulled one, and it has the added advantage of leaving your horse with the protection that Nature intended. You need a full tail to work on; if your horse's tail has been pulled, you will have to be patient and put up with the awful 'growing out' stage until the hairs are long enough to take into a plait.

Take a small section of hair from each side of the tail at the top and cross them over, then take a third section from the side to the centre. Tail plaiting utilises a similar technique to that needed for running plaits, but this time you take in a section from each side every time you cross over the centre one. The keynotes to getting a good result are to only take in a few hairs from the side each time, and to keep your plait tight from the top.

If you pass the side sections over the top of the centre one each time, you will make a flat plait. If you pass them underneath, your centre plait will stand out in relief. Most horses look best if the plait reaches about two-thirds of the way down the dock; when you reach the appropriate point, carry on plaiting so that you end up with one long plait, then fasten the end and double it up.

Whenever possible, plait manes and tails on the morning of a show rather than the night before, or you may find that your handiwork is coming undone or is covered with bits of bedding next morning. Bandage a plaited tail as normal for travelling, but remember to unwind the bandage rather than pulling it off in one go – if you forget, you may pull out your plait at the same time.

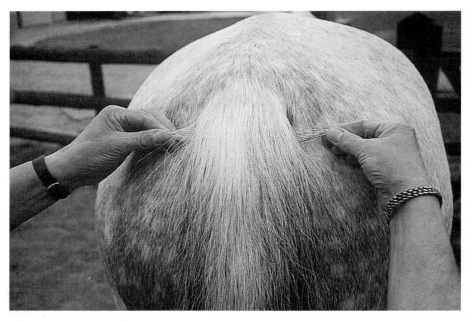

Step by step to a perfectly plaited tail. There are two techniques, one where the central plait lies flat and the other – shown here – which results in a raised plait.

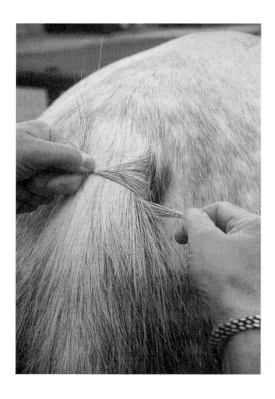

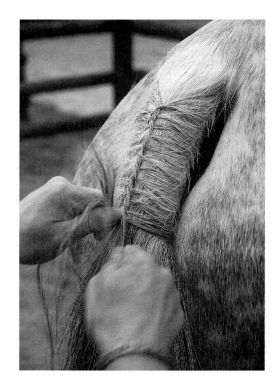

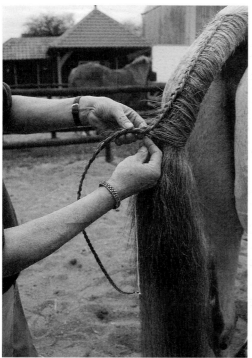

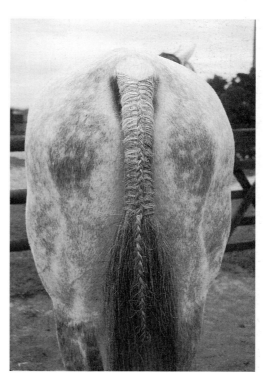

Clipping

When your horse looks like an overgrown pony with a woolly coat and hairy chin, it is tempting to reach for the clippers and transform him. But whilst clipping a horse makes him look much smarter, remember that this is not the prime object of the exercise. First and foremost, you are aiming to help him work comfortably by lessening the risk of him sweating too much.

Think twice before you take off all his coat. A full clip may look nice, but is only suitable for a horse in really hard work who is turned out for relaxation. The horse or pony in light to medium work should be left with protection over his back and loins and the one who lives out all or most of the time should be given a minimal clip. For animals in the first category, a trace clip, chaser clip or low blanket clip is a good option; horses who live out should not be given more than a bib clip, where the hair is clipped from the throat and front of the chest.

Clipping, like plaiting, takes practice. If possible, learn the basic techniques on a horse who stays calm and is easy to handle; if you and your horse are new to clipping, or you think he might be difficult, get someone experienced and confident to do it the first few times. It is asking for trouble if horse and rider are both unsure of themselves.

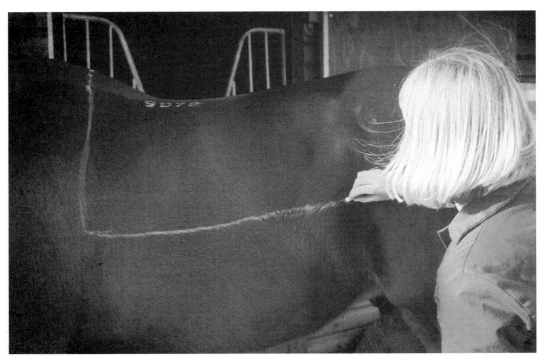

Drawing chalk lines can help decide where to position clips such as blanket and trace clips.

Safety first

As long as you keep your wits about you and use your common sense, you should be able to clip your horse safely. However, there are things to watch out for, especially if you are using electric clippers or if you are dealing with a nervous or potentially difficult horse. Keep the following safety code in mind:

- If you are using electric clippers, always use a circuit breaker at the socket. Place extension leads where the horse is unlikely to tread on them.
- If you are unsure of your horse's reactions, or if he is ticklish, wear a hard hat or skull cap whilst you are clipping. It could save you from injury if, for instance, he cow kicks whilst you are clipping his belly.
- Choose the time and place carefully. You need a dry, light area out of the wind – by all means tie him up outside his stable in a quiet yard, but do not attempt to clip if it is windy or raining, if there are things going on that might unsettle him, or if he is expecting to be fed. If you clip him in his stable, pile up the bedding round the edges so that you can sweep up the hair that comes off.
- Battery-operated clippers are usually quieter than electric ones, which can be helpful when dealing with nervous or inexperienced horses, but not all battery clippers are powerful enough to cope with anything more than minimal clips. Clippers which run off a car battery are a useful alternative.
- Watch your horse's reactions whilst you are working. No matter how well behaved he is, do not take his good behaviour for granted – if you do, chances are that this is the one occasion when he spooks or objects to something!
- Keep your clippers clean, cool and well lubricated. Check the manufacturer's instructions for tensioning the blades correctly, cleaning and maintenance.
- Never put clippers straight on to the horse, even if he is used to the process. Switch them on so that he gets used to the noise, then put your hand on his shoulder and rest the clippers on your hand so that he accepts the muted vibration. Rest the clippers on him so that he feels the direct vibration, then start clipping in a less sensitive area – the shoulder is often a good place.

Difficult areas

Clipping large areas of the horse's body is not too difficult; it is areas such as the top of the legs, the stifle and the head that catch most people out. In most cases, it is sensible to leave the hair on the legs as protection, though some people clip the legs right out first time round and then leave on the resulting re-growth.

The simplest way of deciding where to draw the line at the tops of the legs is to simply follow the lines of muscles. Your clip at the top of the forelegs should look like an upside-down V, whilst on the hindlegs it should slope up towards the stifle. If it makes you feel more confident, draw guidelines with chalk.

Chalk lines are the best way of working out where the level of a blanket or trace clip should fall. If you are not sure, start off with a low clip – you can always take a bit more off later. Where lines on each side meet up at the withers, use a piece of string to ensure a neat join . . . it is really irritating to ride along looking down on a lopsided blanket clip!

Be prepared to stretch the horse's skin gently with your fingers to get into awkward areas more easily. You will be clipping against the direction of the hair, which some-times means altering the angle of the clippers. At the stifle, for instance, the hair radiates out, so you need to turn the clippers to follow the natural curve.

You can either clip your horse's head right out or clip up to a line from the base of his ear to the corner of his mouth. Many people clip heads with no problems, but it is not something to attempt with a nervous or difficult horse as it necessitates clipping the eye area. The second option is less risky and looks smart enough for most purposes, as it gives a sharper outline to the jaw.

Ears are another potential problem area. Some horses are not bothered, others will only tolerate small battery-powered clippers and some do not want clippers near their ears at any cost. Be patient and do not take risks; I had one horse who started off refusing to allow clippers anywhere near his ears, but four years and twelve clips later he was calm enough to allow us to trim them.

All you are trying to do is give a neater outline. It is not fair to shave all the hair from inside the ears, as is sometimes seen – it is there to act as a filter and lessen the risk of hay seeds and other foreign bodies dropping inside the area and setting up irritation. If your horse really hates clippers near his ears, compromise by using a small pair of round-ended scissors: gently close the edges of the ear together and trim off the hair at the outside edges.

Handling difficult horses

Some horses accept being clipped as easily as they accept being groomed. Others are nervous to start with, but gain confidence as long as they are treated with the right mix of kindness and firmness. A few are always difficult and a handful are downright impossible!

If you are dealing with a horse who has never been clipped before, or who is an unknown quantity, introduce the clippers gradually, as explained in the section on safety. It is often better to hold difficult horses rather than tie them up; both clipper and helper must be able to stay calm. Putting a bridle on the horse gives more control than if he is wearing a headcollar.

Both clipper and helper should stand on the same side of the horse. If he becomes frightened or 'bolshy', he will move away from the clippers – and if the helper is standing on the opposite side, he or she is likely to get trodden on. When possible, keep the horse's head turned slightly towards the side being clipped. If he moves, his quarters will then swing away from the person clipping.

Some horses stamp or kick when their legs are being trimmed. If he objects to having a foreleg trimmed, the helper should pick up the other foreleg. When he dislikes clippers being used on a hindleg, the answer is to pick up the foreleg on the same side: for instance, if you are having problems trimming his near hindleg, your helper should hold up his near fore.

Using a twitch has a calming effect on many horses. As long as it is used correctly, which means only on the upper lip, it does not hurt the horse – especially if you use a metal humane twitch. Vets say that this device works not by causing the horse pain, but by stimulating the production of endorphins, natural relaxants which induce a feeling of calmness. With some horses, the calming effect is so marked that they nearly fall asleep.

Occasionally you come across a horse who does not seem to create his own endorphins in response to a twitch. In this case, you have two alternatives: either ask your vet to come out and sedate him, or start rugging him up at the end of August to try and inhibit the growth of his winter coat. Modern sedatives are effective, but the person clipping needs to be able to work fast and efficiently.

Hand clippers are available, but tend to be small and not exactly quick to use. However, if you have the time and patience they can be used to take off a small amount of coat on the horse's chest and throat, which could mean the difference between being able to work him gently or having to cope with a sweaty coat after even light exercise.

Chapter 8
Tack and Clothing

Equipping your horse with tack, rugs, boots and other equipment is seriously expensive. If you buy everything new, you can run up a bill of £2,000 without even trying. A good saddle will be anything from £500 – £1,000-plus, depending on quality, whilst a well-designed New Zealand rug will be £100 – £200-plus.

There are ways to cut costs, but you have to be careful and accept that getting long-term value does not necessarily equate with buying the cheapest equipment. Think of it in terms of cost per use: an £80 rug that proves to be a bad buy because it slips, or has poor quality fastenings which break, will work out more expensive than a £150 one which lasts three years and does the job for which it is designed.

Buying secondhand tack is another way of keeping down your expenses, but this takes skill and luck, particularly with saddles. If you buy from a reputable saddler, you should get a guarantee that equipment has been checked and if necessary repaired before being re-sold; if you buy a saddle advertised in the local paper by a private owner, you could face problems if it turns out to be defective.

Buying tack and rugs secondhand carries with it a slight risk that the previous wearer had a skin infection such as ringworm. You would admittedly have to be very unlucky for this to be the case, but may prefer to play safe by washing equipment in solutions designed to combat ringworm before using it on your horse.

Saddle up

Your saddle is a major investment, in terms of your horse's and your own comfort as well as money. Most owners are aware of how important it is that a saddle fits correctly, but putting theory into practice is not always easy. There are other questions to think about, too.

Unless you have the money to buy different designs for different purposes – for example, a dressage saddle for schooling on the flat and a general purpose or jumping saddle for work over fences – how do you decide which one will suit you best? If it fits your horse, will it also fit you? What do you do if you have a horse who is likely to grow or change shape as he muscles up? Can you use the same saddle on more than one horse?

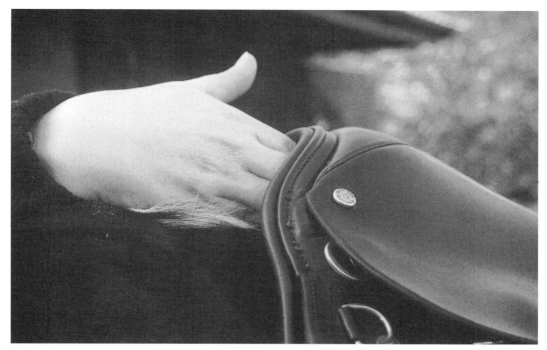

Check with a rider on board that there is sufficient clearance under the front of the saddle.

Fit for both of you

It is easy enough to say that only experts should fit saddles, and much more difficult to find them. Neither retailers nor saddle makers are automatically experts in fitting, though you may be lucky and find someone who qualifies on all counts. The Society of Master Saddlers has made a brave attempt to solve this problem by running saddle fitting courses for its members, where participants cover everything from horse anatomy to saddle design and have to prove their competence to gain the society's certificate.

Starting off with a well-fitting saddle is only the beginning of the story. The ultimate responsibility lies with you and you have to learn to check your saddle and recognise when you might need to call back your expert to have it adjusted or even changed. Malan Goddard, a master saddler and former lecturer at Cordwainer's College, London, says that every horse and saddle should be checked by the owner once a month. This DIY action plan incorporates her advice:

(a) The definition of a well-fitting saddle is one which follows the profile of the horse's back, distributes the rider's weight over as wide an area as possible and does not interfere with the horse's movement. It must also help you to ride in a correct and comfortable position; if your saddle puts you out of balance, your horse will suffer.

(b) A horse should only be ridden if he is sound and free from any signs of pain and discomfort. Obviously this applies to the areas which bear the weight of saddle and rider, but saddle fit can be affected by other problems. For instance, if a horse has a problem in his hock he may carry himself awkwardly to try and relieve discomfort, thus unbalancing his rider's weight and creating pressure points that, strictly speaking, are not the fault of the saddle.

Run your hands along the horse's back to check for signs of soreness or tightness, keeping your touch firm but consistent. If someone suddenly dug their fingers in your back, you would object! The most vulnerable areas are just below the withers, where the points of a tree which is too narrow dig in, and at the back of the saddle. The commonest problem is a tree which is too narrow.

(c) Put the saddle on the horse, without a numnah, pad or saddle cloth. Make sure it is far enough back not to interfere with the movement of his shoulder – the top of the shoulder blade rotates backwards up to three inches with every stride. Tighten the girth gently and gradually: you should finish by being able to fit the flat of your fingers between the girth and the horse's side, and his skin should not be pinched or wrinkled.

(d) The tree must be the correct width and profile for the horse's back. To get a picture of your horse's shape, buy an architect's Flexicurve (an aid for drawing curved lines) from a stationer's. Place it over the horse's withers behind the shoulder, where the front arch of the saddle rests, and mould it to his shape. Draw inside it and use the resultant shape to gauge the correct saddle width.

(e) The saddle should follow the shape of the horse's back so that as wide an area as possible of the underneath is in contact.

(f) When you are on board, there must be adequate clearance of the withers and all along the gullet. The textbook advice is that there should be three fingers' width between the withers and the front arch, but there is some leeway. Certainly there must be one finger's clearance when you stand in the stirrups. You need more leeway if you are going to jump than if your horse always keeps four feet on the ground.

(g) The saddle should sit central, not tip to one side. Remember that a lopsided rider can pull the saddle over, so get someone to check that you sit square.

(h) There is bound to be some movement, but it should not be obvious. If the saddle bounces up and down or swings from side to side, you have a problem.

(i) Check the saddle with the rider on board, before the horse starts work, and during and after work in all paces on both reins.

(j) When you look at your saddle from the side, it should be level and the deepest part of the seat should be in the centre. If it looks as if it is going uphill or down-hill, you will be tipped out of balance.

(k) If you want to use a numnah, tell your saddle fitter. Most say that a thin numnah is better than a thick one, as the latter can make a correctly fitting saddle too tight. Numnahs and pads cannot turn a badly fitting saddle into one which fits well, though research data on some of the latest designs seems to show that they can help give a better bearing surface.

Using a Flexicurve to take a wither profile.

(1)   Ideally, every horse should have his own saddle. This is obviously impossible in dealing yards and many professional riders prefer riding on one design and are reluctant to accept that it may not suit all horses – an attitude not always in the horse's best interests. The Reactorpanel saddle (see next section) usually offers a solution for riders who have to use the same saddle on more than one horse.

Fitting the rider

Your saddle needs to fit you as well as your horse, which means that your physiques should ideally complement one another. You can overcome the problem of a small rider on a large horse by riding on a saddle that is theoretically a little too big, but a large rider on a small horse is more difficult. If the seat has to be so large to accommodate the rider's backside that it puts pressure too far back on the horse, you will cause discomfort and eventual damage . . . so the rider has to either put up with a slightly too small seat, or find a bigger horse.

Your saddle should help you stay in balance, so its proportions should suit yours. Flaps that are the wrong length will catch on the top of long riding boots, whilst those that are designed so that your thighs hang over them at the back will lessen your comfort.

Most saddles have knee rolls and some also have thigh rolls. These should help your position, not lock you in a vice – for instance, your knees should be just behind the knee rolls when your stirrups are at the appropriate length. Some saddles have movable knee and thigh blocks which fasten with heavy-duty Velcro.

The positioning of the stirrup bars ties in with getting the right balance. Fortunately, more manufacturers are now aware of this. If the bars are set too far forwards, which used to be a common design fault and is still something to watch out for, you will be constantly drawing your leg back to achieve the right position and thus putting yourself off balance. Adjustable stirrup bars allow you to alter the position according to the activity and the rider's ability, so on a general purpose saddle you could, in theory, position them farther forwards for jumping than for flatwork.

Unless you are a specialist and therefore only wish to ride on a dressage or jumping saddle, you will probably aim for a general purpose (GP) model. Inevitably, the GP has to be a jack of all trades and designs vary between manufacturers. Some are more forward cut than others, so would be more suitable for the rider who wants to do a fair amount of jumping.

In an attempt to overcome this problem, some designers have produced saddles deliberately slanted more to one style of riding than the other. If you want to school, hack, show and jump smaller courses up to about three foot, look for saddles marketed as GP/D (general purpose/dressage) or VSD (very slightly dressage). Movable knee rolls give more flexibility.

Albion's Selecta is an ingenious attempt to give several options within a single saddle, via interchangeable flaps. These have a special fixing system which ensures that they do not come off accidentally.

Fitting difficult horses

Horses, like people, come in different shapes and sizes. A horse with good conformation makes a saddle fitter's job easier – but no horse is perfect, and most problems can be overcome. Saddler and inventor Barry Richardson has spent nearly thirty years making and fitting saddles and studying conformation, and has yet to be defeated.

Barry believes that it is not really fair to talk about conformation problems; he prefers to think in terms of how the horse is shaped and how the saddle can be adapted. He has identified some common challenges and strategies for dealing with them:

- All horses have a natural girth groove and the girth will settle into the narrowest part of the horse's belly. If the groove is too close to the elbow you may get soreness in that area and many saddles will tend to move forwards – particularly if the horse's shoulder is upright rather than sloping.

   If the problem is mild, using a 'Limpet pad©' under the saddle may be the answer. These work effectively when they are damp, so in winter, when the horse is less likely to sweat, you may need to dampen the pad or sponge the horse with warm water before saddling up.

Point straps, extra girth straps fitted below the points of the tree, also help. Best results are usually obtained if both the point straps and the ordinary girth straps are anchored as low as possible.

If the girth groove is too far back, breastplates and breastgirths are acceptable for every discipline except showing. The straps must be wide, to keep the horse comfortable, and they should be fitted carefully. It may also help if your girth straps are well to the rear of the sweat flaps.

- If your horse has a straight back, he needs a saddle with a tree profile to match – the sort used in close contact, flat seated jumping saddles and in some showing saddles. The problem is that some riders say they cannot ride on them, mainly because they have been relying on the false security of a so-called 'deep-seated' saddle.
- These 'deep-seated' saddles are the answer for the horse with the opposite problem the curved or sway back. Again, you are following the rule that the tree profile must follow that of the horse's back.

If you try to use a saddle with a curved tree on a horse with a straight or 'normal' back, it will rock and cause pressure problems.

Barry became so fascinated with problems posed by fitting saddles that he designed what he believes is the closest to perfection. His Reactorpanel saddle, which has flexible, movable panels fixed with Sorbethane blocks, gives the greatest possible weight bearing area.

The standard set-up suits most horses, but the panels can be moved to suit wide degrees of asymmetry and curvature. Unlike conventional saddles, the Reactorpanel never needs re-flocking – the panels contain high-tech plastic which flexes with the horse's movements. As long as the basic tree width is correct, you can use this saddle on any number of horses.

Tests with the Saddletech system, a pressure pad linked to a computer which shows precisely what is happening underneath the saddle, give excellent ratings. Riding on a Reactorpanel gives a different 'feel' from that of an ordinary saddle, so you have to be prepared to get used to it.

Buying secondhand

The golden rule about buying tack is to always go for the best you can afford. If your spending power is limited, you may find that in some cases – particularly saddles – buying secondhand is an attractive option. It can also be risky, especially if you buy at auction or from someone who has no proof of the equipment's origins.

Buying secondhand from a reputable retailer or saddler is the safest way. Many take saddles in part exchange against new ones, usually when owners sell a horse and find

The Reactorpanel saddle has brought new thinking to saddle fitting. It has flexible, movable panels that do away with the need for re-flocking and mean that as long as the basic tree width is correct, the saddle can be used on different horses.

that their old saddle does not fit their next purchase. As long as the retailer knows where it has come from and has checked it for possible damage, this is usually a good bet.

You will usually pay more than if you had bought privately, because a saddler/retailer has to cost in overheads and is also in business to make a profit, but you may feel that the safeguards are worth the extra. Some saddlers will include free fitting and adjustment as part of the price, whilst others will make a charge. As always, make sure that the person who offers to fit the saddle knows what he or she is doing.

Buying privately, perhaps from an advertisement in a local paper or national horse magazine, may be cheaper but comes with more potential pitfalls. For a start, can you be sure that the tack is not stolen? If the seller cannot provide proof of purchase – and

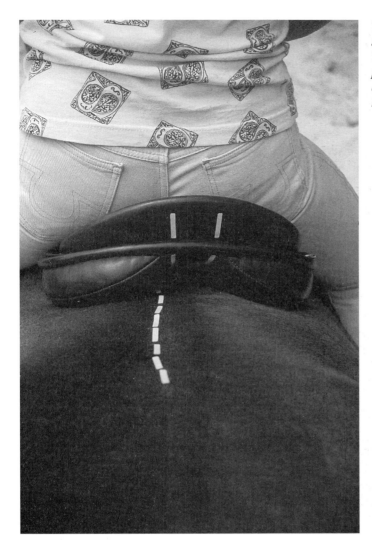

The tape line shows how this saddle has moved to one side. This will inevitably cause pressure points, discomfort and even long-term damage to the horse.

a genuine one may have lost or not kept a receipt, especially if it was not new when they bought it – do you take the goods on face value?

This may seem over cautious, but things do go wrong. I once had a saddle stolen that both I and the maker could identify. Two years later, I saw an advertisement for a saddle that sounded remarkably like mine. It was, though the advertiser had bought it in good faith from a tack 'boot sale'. The upshot was that it was taken by police, identified by me and returned to my insurance company, who had paid for its loss. The advertiser's only possible recourse was against the person she had bought it from, but she did not know their identity.

As a saddle is only of use if it will fit your horse, you usually have to take a chance and be prepared to sell it again if it proves unsuitable. Some people will let you take your horse and try it, which means you have to be able to trust your own judgement, or will agree to refund your money if the saddle is returned in the same condition within a certain period.

This sounds fine, but it can go wrong. I know someone who bought a dressage saddle for £275 on condition that she could return it within twenty-four hours. It turned out to be slightly too narrow, but when she took it back the seller – a seemingly charming woman who had asked for payment in cash – claimed that there were new scratches on the pommel.

The written agreement specified, quite fairly, that the saddle must be returned in the same condition. She refused to take it back and the buyer had the choice of either taking action against her through the small claims court or selling the saddle to try and recoup her loss. She decided that the second course was the quickest way to avoid more complications and lost £25.

Buying at auction will probably give you the lowest prices of all, as long as you are not carried away by the atmosphere and the bidding and end up paying more than you intended to! But what you see is what you get; you are deemed to have inspected the goods beforehand and if you get a saddle or bridle home and find that you missed some broken stitching or a split in the leather, it is your hard luck. You may, of course, notice minor damage but manage to buy the tack at a price low enough to justify the cost of repairs.

The same guidelines apply to buying at equestrian 'boot fairs', which have become increasingly common. From the seller's point of view, they can be a good way of getting rid of unwanted items and raising extra cash to pay for other things. If you go along as a buyer, be just as careful as if you were buying at auction.

Checking the goods

Inspect secondhand goods as thoroughly as possible, looking for identification marks as well as signs of weakness and damage. If a saddle is marked with a postcode, is it the same as the vendor's . . . and if not, should warning bells ring? It could be, of course, that the vendor has moved house since originally buying and marking the saddle, or bought it secondhand. But it could also mean that the tack is stolen.

With saddles, the most important thing is to try and find out whether the tree is sound. Malan Goddard recommends the following checks:

(a) Put it on a flat surface, such as a table, with the seat facing upwards. Place a hand on each point pocket, under the flaps, and squeeze hard. If there are any grinding noises and/or you can push the tree points in easily, suspect a problem.

(b) Hold the saddle with the cantle tucked into your stomach and pull the pommel towards you. With a spring tree saddle, you expect a certain amount of give – but if there is obvious creasing of the seat, or the saddle looks twisted or lopsided, it is likely that the tree is broken.

Unfortunately, some damage can only be seen by taking the saddle apart and inspecting the tree. If you have the slightest suspicion, do not buy the saddle.

Minor problems can be put right by a good saddler. Check down the centre of the gullet and look for unevenness, which may indicate that the stitching holding the panel together has come loose, and run your hand lightly over the panel to check for bumps and hollows. If the panel is wool flocked, you can get hard lumps which will cause pressure points and discomfort for your horse.

Are the girth straps in good condition? These take a lot of strain, though they can obviously be replaced. Check the stitching at the top.

All leather should be checked for signs of damage. Look at areas where metal rests on leather – where cheekpieces and reins fasten to bit rings and where stirrup leathers

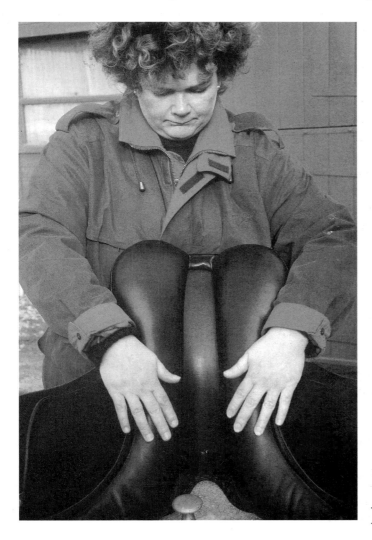

Master saddler Malan Goddard, a specialist saddle fitter, checks for uneven flocking.

bear the irons. Check stitching, too, particularly on reins and stirrup leathers. If it comes apart when you give it a good tug, it is not safe . . . and if the vendor objects, point out that you have just prevented a potentially nasty accident!

Buckle holes should be clean, with no cracks or splits surrounding them. Leather in general should be reasonably soft and supple; if it feels stiff and dry it has either been dried out too quickly after a soaking or not looked after properly.

Synthetic tack

When synthetic tack first came on the market it was cheap and, it has to be said, fairly nasty! Since then, materials and designs have improved enormously and many endurance riders use synthetic tack, particularly bridles, as a matter of choice.

The advantages are that it is usually cheaper to buy in the first place and quicker and easier to clean. The disadvantages are that it does not last as long as well cared for leather tack and most riders do not find it as smart.

With synthetic saddles, the biggest danger is the misconception that because they are much lighter than leather ones, they cannot harm the horse's back. The reality is that they can cause just as much damage if they are not fitted and adjusted with the same care and precision. Early models had narrow panels and gullets, which meant that achieving correct clearance and a wide bearing surface was virtually impossible, but many modern designs are much better.

The latest generation of synthetic saddles is much closer to leather in appearance than their predecessors. One manufacturer says that this has caused him problems, because people assume that they should use saddle soap and leather dressings on them, which damages the material. Follow the manufacturer's instructions and you will not damage your saddle or embarrass yourself!

Bit basics

There are so many designs of bit and so many choices of mouthpiece material that many riders can end up totally confused. Bitting is dealt with in depth in *Tack: How to Choose It and Use It*, also by Carolyn Henderson and published by Swan Hill Press – but this section is a brief survivors' guide to the bitting minefield.

For many riders, the biggest question is simply what bit they should use on their horse. Most prefer to use some sort of snaffle, either because they want to compete in the lower levels of dressage and are bound by competition rules, or because they feel it is the mildest form of bit.

As long as you use the right snaffle for your particular horse – and just as important, as long as the reins are in the right hands – a snaffle is an excellent bit. But if you are using an unsuitable mouthpiece, or if your horse would actually be more comfortable

Two modern synthetic saddles – the one on the left by Jabez Cliff, the other by Thorowgood – which prove that synthetic need not be synonymous with cheap and nasty. However, just as much care must be taken with fitting.

and would therefore go better in a bit with a curb action, you need to re-think your approach.

For a start, the premise that a bit is always milder if it has a fat mouthpiece is a generalisation, not a rule. A fat mouthpiece gives a broader bearing surface, but if the horse's mouth cannot accommodate it, or the rider has to use strong rein aids, it is not necessarily the kindest option.

If you have a problem, or think that your horse would go better in a different bit, always go back to basics and get his mouth and teeth checked to make sure that they are in good condition. Changing the bit will make no difference if he has sharp edges on his teeth, or wolf teeth are interfering with its action.

Do not assume that having your horse's teeth rasped once a year is always sufficient. Some horses need attention twice a year or even more frequently, especially three- to five-year-olds who are being asked to work whilst their mouths are in a state of constant change.

Some vets are excellent at sorting out mouth and teeth problems and appreciate the importance of correct dental care. Others, unfortunately, seem to think that a ten-second rasp without the use of a gag to hold the horse's mouth open and allow maximum access is sufficient. For this reason, many owners prefer to use specialist equine dental technicians: they are usually referred to as dentists, but this is colloquial rather than strictly correct terminology.

Check that your riding is not compounding or even causing problems. For instance, is the horse leaning on the bit because he is on his forehand? If so, transitions and half-halts will help.

Look at the shape of your horse's mouth and tongue before using the first snaffle that comes to hand. If he cannot close his mouth round a thick mouthpiece, use a thinner one. If he has a thick tongue, he will often be happier with a French link snaffle (which has a kidney-shaped central link) than a single jointed mouthpiece.

Do you have to use a snaffle? Some horses seem to take much more kindly to a pelham, used with two pairs of reins. One reason may be that they simply find it more comfortable and respond well to the combination of poll pressure and mild curb action. Another is that riders tend to ride more sensitively when using a pelham, which the horse appreciates.

If you want to stick to the snaffle family, you have a huge range of mouthpiece materials and cheekpiece designs to choose from. In particular, there has been a huge surge in popularity of materials which encourage the horse to salivate and (hopefully) relax the lower jaw. These include sweet iron bits and alloys incorporating copper, and many horses seem to like them. American bits incorporating sweet iron and copper are particularly successful; they are said to give a combination of 'sweet and sour' tastes and horses react well to them.

Your choice of bit alone will rarely solve a problem, as there are so many other things to take into account. However, it is an important part of the overall picture. For that reason, the following suggestions may act as guidelines for riders coping with particular problems.

Problem: Dry, unresponsive mouth.
Solution: Check that the horse's mouth can accommodate the mouthpiece. If he does not have room for a thick mouthpiece and his mouth is permanently open, it will also be dry. Try a thinner mouthpiece and/or a French link snaffle.

Use a bit with a sweet iron or copper alloy mouthpiece. Look for names like Sprenger, Aurigan, Kangaroo, Cyprium and sweet iron. In Britain, Equine America markets bits incorporating sweet iron and copper. If you compete in dressage, remember that unfortunately, the current rule book states that all parts of the bit which go in the horse's mouth must be made from the same material.

Problem: Above the bit.
Solution: A loose ring snaffle, whose mouthpiece continually makes tiny movements in the horse's mouth, is preferable to a 'fixed' bit such as an eggbutt, which stays relatively still in the mouth.

Problem: Behind the bit.
Solution: This is the opposite scenario. Try a bit which stays still and gives the horse confidence to accept a contact, such as an eggbutt or full cheek.

Problem: Leaning on the bit.
Solution: Use a bit with loose rings, perhaps coupled with rollers set around the mouthpiece.

Problem: No brakes.
Solution: Get help from someone who can explain riding techniques rather than use brute strength. In any case, a horse is far stronger than any rider. This problem may demand a back to basics approach on your horse's schooling, particularly if he is on his forehand or associates the bit with pain because of previous rough riding.

Changing from a snaffle to a pelham with double reins often gives good results, as horses tend to come off their forehand and be lighter to ride. Event riders favour three-ring snaffles with the reins on the lowest ring. Sweet iron bits with 'scrub boards' —small ridges set in the mouthpieces, not to be confused with the much more severe twisted mouthpieces – work well with some horses.

Problem: No steering.
Solution: A bit with full cheeks or D-rings is often useful, especially with young horses. Alternatively, rubber bitguards prevent the bit rings being pulled into the mouth, and cushion the sides.

Problem: Tongue over the bit.
Solution: Double check that the bit is the right size and is adjusted high enough in the horse's mouth. With a jointed mouthpiece, gently straighten it in the horse's mouth by hooking your thumbs through the bit rings. You should be able to fit *no more* than the width of a finger between the bit rings and the corners of the horse's mouth on each side.

The bit should be adjusted high enough to fit snugly in the corners of the mouth. If the horse has a fleshy mouth, this may produce a wrinkle at each side – and if you are in doubt, opt for a higher rather than a lower adjustment.

The type of bit you use can also help. Some horses dislike tongue pressure and are happier with bits that are suspended in their mouth, such as pelhams, kimblewicks and hanging cheek snaffles. A mullen mouthed bit or one with a small port may also do the trick. If your horse goes well in a snaffle with full cheeks, use keepers at the top of the cheeks to fasten the bit cheeks to the bridle cheekpieces. This means that the joint rests higher in the mouth than if the bit is used without keepers.

I once had a young horse who had been backed using a bit that was too big, and he constantly drew back his tongue and tried to put it over the bit even when equipped with one the correct size. He stopped doing it when he was ridden in a jointed snaffle with alternate copper and steel rollers.

Metal tongue grids and rubber tongue ports are designed to prevent the horse drawing his tongue far enough back to get it over the bit. They may work with some horses, but others manage to overcome them. The old-fashioned 'nagbutt' or 'butterfly' bit has spatulas incorporated in the centre of the mouthpiece designed to lay the tongue flat. Some horses accept them, but others hate them so much they refuse to go forwards or even rear.

Some people will tell you to use a tightly fastened Flash or drop noseband, their reasoning being that if the horse cannot open his mouth, he cannot put his tongue over the bit. But if his mouth is strapped shut, he will not be able to relax his jaw and as a result cannot be expected to work happily or correctly. There is also the risk that a determined horse will manage to put his tongue over the bit, then panic when he cannot get it back under the mouthpiece.

The tongue helps to act as a cushion between the mouthpiece and the bars of the mouth, so if that cushion is removed, the action is more severe. Unfortunately, some horses do not seem to work out that they are more comfortable with the bit where it is supposed to be.

I know of one rider who tried all the above methods, without success. In desperation, she used a flexible plastic snaffle and let the horse put his tongue over it. He went quite happily and was even placed in dressage tests; none of the judges ever realised that he was performing his test with his tongue over the bit!

Rugs

Rugs are essential for most horses and ponies, at least in winter. The only exceptions are some native ponies, whose coats provide excellent insulation – though as soon as they are clipped, which is essential for any pony doing all but the lightest work, you have to rug them up to compensate. As always, even the unclipped pony must have adequate shelter.

Rug materials and designs have changed dramatically over the last few years. This means that though they are relatively more expensive, they are also more effective and in many cases, more versatile. If you want to get maximum value for money, think about the following points:

- Is it well designed so that it stays in place without rubbing?
- Will it do the job – or preferably, more than one job? A £60 New Zealand that lets water through seams is a waste of money. A £150 lightweight rug

This Wug by Ireland Horseware incorporates a neck cover and tail flap, giving protection at both ends. It is light, breathable and waterproof and can be used indoors and out.

that is totally waterproof and can be used indoors and out can be a good buy.
- Is it easy to keep clean? A lightweight, machine washable rug that keeps your horse as warm and dry as a heavier one is easier to handle and dry off.

Rugs are often sold secondhand, usually when someone sells a horse or pony and buys another who needs a different size. You run a risk that the previous wearer had a skin infection, but washing it before use in products developed to 'kill' ringworm should make it safe.

Better by design

Horses come in all shapes and sizes and some are more difficult to fit with rugs than others. Cobs, for instance, have deep, broad bodies on short legs and measuring them the conventional way – from the centre of the chest along the full length of the body – will often result in a rug that is the correct length over the back, but too tight in the front.

However, if you look for rugs which are cut high on the neck, you will solve nearly all fitting problems. This is the design keynote, because if the rug is cut high enough it

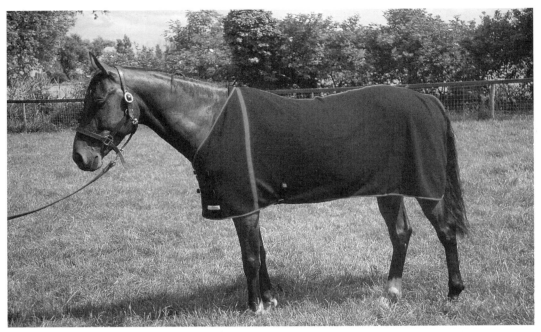

This thermal rug by Thermatex transfers moisture from the horse's body to the outer surface of the rug and can be put on a wet or sweating horse.

will not slip back. You can also usually buy a size larger than usual to compensate for a broad chest.

Horseware has gone one step farther with its Wug, a rug that also incorporates a neck cover. The front fastenings are set at an angle to make sure that they take the strain easily without causing pressure points, and the extra fabric over the neck means that you do not get rubbing at the base of the mane, as can happen with conventional necklines.

Fastenings also affect fit. Cross surcingles are the commonest and as long as they are adjusted correctly – so that they cross in the centre of the horse's belly, with a hand's width between each surcingle and the horse's body – are effective. Problems can arise if the anchoring points are too narrow, when too much strain is put on too small an area and the rug fabric rips, or when poor quality fastenings rust or break.

'Spider fastenings' are very effective. They comprise a short strap and two longer ones, each with a clip at the end and radiating from a central ring. The short strap clips to the front of the rug and the system passes between the front legs, with the long straps clipping to fastenings at each side. As long as the rug is cut high enough on the neck, it will stay in place with no risk of pressure on the withers or spine.

Knitted thermal fabrics which mould to the horse's shape can also help solve the problem of horses with awkward conformation points, such as high withers. The best designs are bound round the neckline to prevent too much stretching.

Unfortunately, even the nicest horse can be a total thug when it comes to rugs. Even worse, some are no respecters of other horses' rugs. One of the nicest horses I ever had gained great amusement from grabbing hold of his companion's rug and trying to tow him round the field – in fact, it was only the fact that he was so nice in every other way which enabled us to put up with this potentially destructive habit! Any bit of the rug would do, but tailflaps were irresistible.

You cannot expect a rug to be unbreakable. If it was, your horse could be at risk: every rug needs to have a breaking point in case its wearer gets hooked up on something. Nor can you expect rugs to stand up to other horses' hooves and teeth, but as any retailer will tell you, some customers have quite amazing expectations.

How many?

Coolers, turnouts, New Zealands, travel rugs, thermal rugs, stable rugs . . . the list is endless, but how many do you really need? As some styles can cross the boundary between uses, it may be less than you think.

For instance, it used to be accepted that New Zealand rugs were worn outdoors and stable rugs indoors, and that it was essential to change them over as your horse was turned out and brought in. However, new designs and fabrics mean that a rug which protects your horse against the worst of the weather can be just as suitable indoors. It must be removed and replaced at least once a day, so that you can check

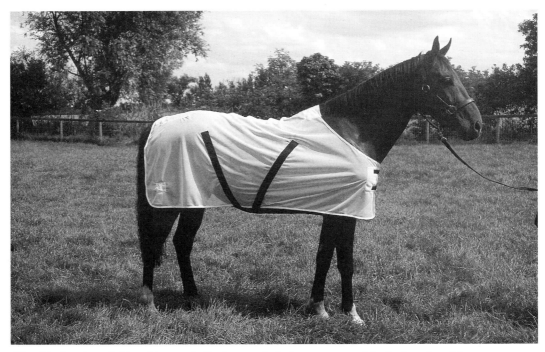

Chaskit developed this white mesh flysheet to help horses cope with the hot, humid, insect-ridden climate of Atlanta for the Olympic Games.

your horse and make sure there are no slight rubs from even gentle pressure on the same points.

If rain does get underneath a rug, it must be replaced and allowed to dry off. You must have at least two New Zealands for each horse, for this reason and also so that if one gets damaged, you have a replacement while it is being mended.

Thermal rugs or coolers are one of those 'how did we manage without them?' developments. They transfer moisture from the horse's body to the outside of the knitted fabric, and so can be put on either a sweating horse or one who has just been bathed. If you want to make an impression, they are smart enough to use for travelling and can be used alone or under other rugs.

The only drawback with knitted fabrics is that bedding, particularly shavings, sticks to them. Thermatex, inventor of the original thermal rug, solved this problem by developing a stable rug with a breathable Cordura outer and a knitted lining. Other companies make lightweight outer rugs which can be used over bulkier, harder to wash styles such as the quilted stable rugs which still have many devotees. Washing these in a domestic washing machine is a lot easier than dealing with a thick quilted rug that may indeed be 'machine washable', but only if your machine is a heavy duty launderette type.

Some horses need protection against the sun as well as the cold and wind. There have been reports of light coloured horses suffering from sunburn; horses of any colour who have been hot branded, notably warmbloods and Lipizzaners, may have the same problem.

If you have to or particularly want to turn your horse out in the daytime, the answer may be to use one of the new lightweight but tough designs developed specifically to combat this. These also help to protect from biting insects. In America, some owners use lightweight leg wraps and say that these deter flies and thus stop horses stamping in irritation. The drawback of using these in hot weather is that if the horse sweats underneath them, the skin may soften and be vulnerable to rubs and irritation.

Alternatively, stable your horse during the day in a well-ventilated stable and turn him out at night, avoiding the danger period of roughly 4–7pm when the biting midges responsible for sweet itch irritation are active. Sunblock products can help minimise the risk of sunburn if you can apply them frequently enough; muzzles and lips are particularly vulnerable.

Master saddler Malan Goddard had a problem with her black Welsh Cob filly, Barley, whose white muzzle was prone to sunburn. She solved the problem by making a 'yashmak' from lightweight fabric which she attached to the noseband of a leather headcollar.

Neck covers and leg wraps are useful timesavers for busy owners. The first keep manes free of mud and are much safer than hoods which cover the whole head, whilst leg wraps can help prevent skin conditions. If your horse comes in with muddy legs, hose them off, dry with a towel and put on thermal leg wraps to dry his legs quickly and efficiently.

This works much better than allowing mud to dry and then brushing it off, which used to be the standard advice. For a start, you may not have time to wait. Even if you do, fungal infections are more likely to develop than if you hosed off and dried his legs.

Cleaning up

Rugs that are machine washable are so easy to keep clean that you have to ask if it is worth buying any other kind. However, it is important to follow the manufacturer's instructions on water temperatures and cleaning agents. Some fabrics have special coatings that are destroyed by ordinary washing powders, and need to be washed using special rug cleaners. If you can use washing powder, make sure you choose the non-biological kind, as some horses are allergic to biological powders.

Small power washers, available from most home/DIY centres, are very efficient and will earn their relatively inexpensive cost many times owner. They are useful for cleaning rugs, mangers and the insides of trailers and horseboxes.

Chapter 9
Reducing the Risks

Keeping a horse is always a risk business. He is not a machine and things can and often do go wrong with him – pick up any horse magazine and you will always find an abundance of articles on veterinary matters. No matter how careful you are, you may still find that things go wrong, and if you cannot accept that, you should not be a horse owner.

At some time, you will have to cope with a crisis. If you are unlucky or own horses for many years, you may have to cope with several crises. This could range from coping with your horse's serious injury or illness to having to make the awful decision to have him put down.

However, although you can never be sure that your horse will not have an accident or that you will not fall victim to horse thieves, there are strategies to ensure that the odds are in your favour. One of the first is to have a horse vetted before you buy him; use a specialist horse vet and if you are buying a horse out of your area, ask your own vet (or the practice you will be using once you have found a horse) to recommend someone.

It is not a good idea to use the vendor's vet, even if he or she has the reputation of being the best in that area – not because the vet is likely to be biased, but because everyone concerned would be in an awkward position if the horse developed problems soon after purchase and you ended up in dispute with the vendor. In any case, the Royal College of Veterinary Surgeons recommends that where possible, a vet declines to vet for purchase a horse belonging to an existing client.

It is important that whoever carries out the vetting must have good experience of equine work. All vets undergo the same basic training, but one who spends most of the time dealing with dogs and cats would arguably not be as suitable as one who specialises in horses.

When you appoint a vet, he will want to know details of the horse for identification if you are unable to be present at the examination. He will also want to know the intended use, so be realistic. Do not tell him that you hope to compete in advanced eventing if you are aiming at riding club one-day events, or he may tell you that the horse is not suitable for your purpose when it may have been ideal.

Some vets ask what price you have agreed to pay, though strictly speaking, this is a matter between vendor and purchaser. The vet may think that you have found a

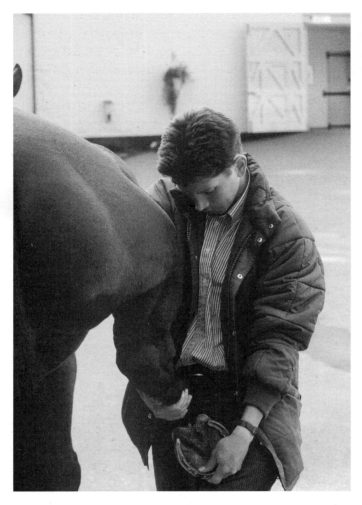

Having a horse vetted by a specialist equine vet can save you heartbreak and money. Andy Bathe is equine surgeon at Cambridge University Veterinary School and vet to the British three-day event team.

bargain or are paying through the nose, but that should have no bearing on his findings. Similarly, if the horse is said to be free from vices and allergies, it is up to you to get a written warranty from the seller. The vet may ask if this is the case, and it is a good idea to request him to do so, but they are not amongst the areas covered by the vetting.

A lot of people misunderstand the true nature of a pre-purchase examination. It is not a guarantee that the horse is a perfect specimen in perfect health and that nothing will go wrong with him in the future. It is the examining veterinary surgeon's opinion that there are 'no clinically discoverable signs of disease, injury or physical abnormality other than those here reported' which 'on the balance of probabilities' are likely or (hopefully) not likely to prejudice the animal's use for a specified purpose.

You cannot rely on a vendor's veterinary certificate; some people buy horses at auction and offer them for sale a few weeks later, often advertising them 'with vet's certificate'. There are three problems here – the horse may have developed a problem in the meantime, the vetting may not have been done for the same potential use and an insurance company will not accept a certificate from an examination carried out on anyone else's behalf.

Hopefully, a satisfactory vetting means that you can start enjoying yourself with your new horse. Occasionally, things still go wrong. If the horse goes lame two weeks later and you discover that the cause of the problem was in existence at the time of the vetting, your only recourse against the vet was if he was negligent – in other words, if he missed something that he should have spotted. This may all be starting to sound as if a vet's certificate is worth no more than the paper it is written on, but for most people, it represents a good investment.

For a start, it confirms your feeling that the horse is suitable for your purpose: for some people, that peace of mind is valuable. Secondly, it means that if you insure the horse for veterinary fees and six months later he is found to have a progressive condition, you may be able to prove to your insurance company that he was not suffering from it when you bought him.

CASE HISTORY
This case history is included not to make you think that having a horse vetted is a waste of time and money, but to make you aware of the things that can go wrong. Fortunately, it is a rare scenario.

Jane W. bought an unbroken three-year-old from a reputable breeder. He had excellent conformation and paces coupled with a kind temperament and the pre-purchase examination was carried out by an experienced horse vet. He found that the horse was 'unblemished and free from all clinical signs of disease, injury or defect' that would make him suitable for bringing on as an event horse.

Jane took the horse home and started to back him. Five weeks later, he showed occasional lame steps in one hindleg and overnight, developed a thoroughpin – a swelling in the hock area. He was immediately examined and X-rays showed that he had ostechondrosis in that hock, a joint problem which sometimes develops in young horses during periods of rapid growth.

The specialist who analysed the X-rays said that this condition would have been in existence when she bought the horse, though the vendor knew nothing about it and there were no signs that could have been picked up by the vet who made the pre-purchase examination. This meant that veterinary fees insurance cover was invalid, as it was a pre-existing condition – a problem that was in existence when the policy was taken out.

Jane's only recourse was therefore against the vendor, under the Sale of Goods Act. As the stud sold all the horses bred there, it counted as a business and the Act

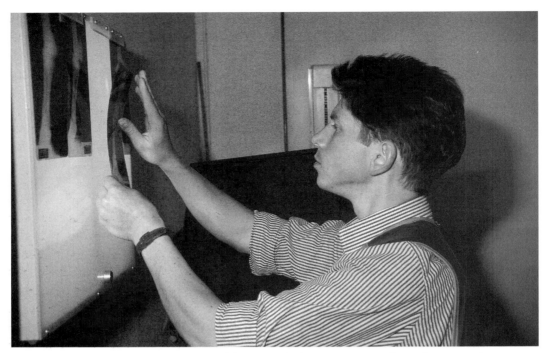

Insurance for veterinary fees can seem like a worthwhile investment if your horse needs expensive diagnostic treatment such as X-rays.

therefore applied. If the horse had been bought from a private seller, protection would have been more limited.

In this sort of case, where an amicable settlement cannot be reached, there are several options. A good starting point is to seek the advice of a solicitor with specialists in equestrian issues; it is a sign of the times that these have become more common in recent years. If you have a straightforward case, a solicitor's letter may do the trick. If you are a member of the British Horse Society, you have access to a free legal helpline which enables you to discuss your problem with a solicitor and decide whether you should take further advice. Most solicitors will, in any case, allow a free initial phone call to assess whether or not you have a potential case and what courses of action are open to you.

The next step, provided your claim is for no more than £3,000, is to take action against the vendor through the small claims court. This is meant to be a user-friendly system and it is possible to take action with or without a solicitor's help. Small claims court staff should advise you. The only drawback is that even if you win your case and an order for payment is made against the other side, it is not always easy to get it enforced if the vendor is reluctant to comply.

Taking action through the county court is the next step up, but this can be a lengthy and costly process that may end up costing you as much as the sum involved – more, if you lose. It is not a step to take without getting specialist legal advice.

If the horse was vetted and you feel that the vet concerned was negligent, you may decide that you have a case against him or her. The vetting procedure is based on a standard procedure and the resulting certificate of examination is phrased in terms of opinions and likelihoods rather than facts; nevertheless, it does not allow for professional negligence.

A sensible policy?

Horse insurance is another complicated and misunderstood area. You may hear all sorts of horror stories about companies which refuse to pay up, but there are two sides to every story. In many cases, the basic problem is that claimants have either not read their policy documents properly or do not understand what the different forms of cover mean. Good companies try and make their policy documents as easy to understand as possible, but they can still be complicated and it is important to read every word of your policy as soon as it arrives. If there is anything you do not understand, ask the person who sold it to you; if you are unhappy with the policy, you can cancel it as long as you do so immediately.

However, it would be naive to assume that insurance companies are anything but businesses run on commercial lines. You may well find yourself dealing with a knowledgeable, sympathetic horse person – and if this is not the case, you have to ask yourself if you have picked the right company – but insurance companies exist to make money.

When you choose insurance cover, you need to know the status of the person who is selling it. You can buy direct from an insurance company or from three kinds of intermediaries: brokers, independent agents or tied agents. There is no rule to say that one is better than another, but you need to know who you are buying from.

Whatever type of policy you decide upon, your horse will be covered for 'the sum insured or market value, whichever is the less.' Do not try and over-insure a horse, as the insurers will not automatically agree that the sum insured and market value are the same thing. In general, when you first take out cover on a new horse it is not worth trying to insure him for more than you paid for him. If his value increases during your ownership, usually because of competition winnings, you can always ask your insurers to increase the sum.

There is no set method of assessing values; some companies use dealers as consultants and will query values which sound as if they could be over-optimistic. It seems logical that if an insurance company accepts the value on your proposal form and takes your premium, then they have agreed with you that this is the horse's market value at the time. You can only insure for actual, not potential, value; you might be certain that your three-year-old will end up as a Grade A show jumper or Grand Prix dressage horse, but you cannot insure dreams.

Most companies offer a choice of cover, starting always with cover for death and theft. This is not as straightforward as many people imagine, often to their cost. You will only be covered for death if the horse dies suddenly, if a vet certifies that immediate destruction is needed on humane grounds or if the insurers give prior consent.

If you decide to have a horse put down, perhaps because he cannot work and you do not want to retire him, you will not be covered unless the insurers give prior consent, which is unlikely. In all cases, the veterinary and disposal costs will usually be down to you, though some policies now include these as part of the cover. You may also be required to pay for a post mortem in some cases, particularly those of sudden death.

Vets' fees

For most owners, cover for veterinary fees is the most important. Vets can do much more now in the way of diagnosis and treatment than even ten years ago, but the result has been an increase in veterinary bills due to the high cost of drugs and diagnostic equipment. For instance, a bone scan could cost £400 – £500 whilst colic surgery will result in a bill for £2,000-plus whether or not the horse survives. A friend whose event horse injured his knee and developed complications ended up with bills approaching £10,000 – fortunately, this sort of scenario is rare.

Insurers will often impose exclusions in future policies on conditions that are likely to arise again. For instance, if your horse has two attacks of colic during one policy period, you will usually find that when the policy comes up for renewal, an exclusion has been placed on it. In other words, you will not be covered for any costs arising out of the horse suffering from colic.

From an owner's point of view, this can seem like a no-win situation. Insurers argue that insurance is there to provide cover against the unexpected, not the likely or the expected! What many owners do not realise is that exclusions are not a once and for all condition: if your horse develops a condition and two or three years later it has not re-occurred, you can ask for the exclusion to be lifted. In theory, a broker acting in your interest should suggest that you do this; in practice, you will probably have to suggest it yourself. Remember that many things are open to negotiation and talk to your insurers – you have nothing to lose and could have something to gain.

When arranging cover for vets' fees, take the following into consideration:

• How much cover are you allowed per incident? You need at least £2,000 if you are to cover the risk of a colic operation or similar, and some people now feel that this is not enough unless you are prepared to top up payments for disasters out of your own pocket.

- Do you have unlimited overall cover for the duration of the policy, or is it limited to a set amount? If you are unlucky enough to have two unrelated sets of large bills in one policy period you could be in trouble.
- Is the veterinary fee cover limited to the sum insured? Some policies may carry a reassuringly large maximum payment per incident, but if the horse is insured for less than a minimum amount will only pay vets' fees up to the sum insured. As costs will be the same regardless of whether the patient is a £50,000 competition horse or a £500 pony, this could cause you problems.
- Is complementary treatment included or do you have to pay a small extra premium? Physiotherapy, remedial shoeing and so on can play an important role in your horse's recovery, but can also be expensive.
- Does cover start from the moment you take out the policy, or is there a waiting period? Some policies do not cover your horse for injury for the first week or fortnight – and when a horse is being introduced to new surroundings and new companions, there is arguably a higher risk that he will get injured.
- Do you pay a standard excess (usually the first £75 – £95) of any bill, however large it is, or do you have to pay an extra percentage over a certain amount?

Loss of use

Loss of use is the most expensive, controversial and misunderstood area of insurance. The official term is 'permanent incapacity,' and the keyword is permanent. If there is a chance that the horse can return to its job after a rest period or treatment, the insurers will want to wait before paying out – which means that in some cases, you may have to wait for up to a year before a final decision can be made.

Most people feel that it is only worth taking out loss of use on a horse who is worth £3,000-plus and who competes, because the likelihood of him being unable to continue as a show jumper, dressage horse, eventer or what have you is much higher than him being unable to hack. It is also the most expensive option: cover for mortality/theft, vets' fees and loss of use on a £3,000 horse used for show jumping and dressage would involve an annual premium of about £350.

Do not assume that if you claim loss of use and your insurers agree, you will automatically be paid the sum insured. The horse always has a residual value, depending on what he is able to do; this can range from carcass value, of perhaps £350, to whatever he is worth according to what he can still do, even if it is only hacking. The insurers will then pay you the difference between the sum insured and the residual value, so if the residual value of your £3,000 horse is deemed to be £1,000, you will receive £2,000.

Deciding the residual value is a matter for negotiation between you and your insurance company. Some are more reasonable than others and a few use dealers, who buy and sell horses all the time, as consultants. If you feel their offer is unfair, say so.

You also need to be very careful that you understand your insurer's terms . . . which comes back to reading the small print in your policy. For instance, some companies make no stipulations regarding the horse's future once loss of use has been agreed and

Horses can look very different before and after they are clipped and trimmed, as this show cob from Lynn Russell's yard shows. Take before and after photographs of your horse for security.

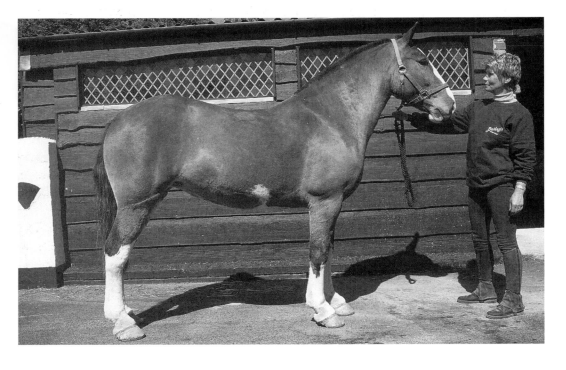

paid, whilst others will only pay a certain percentage unless the animal is destroyed. Some offer a percentage – usually 60 per cent – of the sum insured, less residual value, as standard to keep down the cost of premiums, but will insure for 100 per cent loss of use less residual value if you pay a larger premium.

It is now common practice for insurance companies to stipulate that before loss of use is paid, the horse must be freeze-marked at the owner's expense with the symbol of an L in a circle. If he is not registered with the British Horse Database, this must also be done. This can only be a good idea, as it removes the risk of the horse being sold on to an unwitting buyer and perhaps eventually becoming the subject of another claim with another company. If you are offered a horse freeze-marked in this way, you can check when and why the loss of use claim was made; it may be that he is still suitable for your purpose, though it would be sensible to get veterinary advice.

CASE HISTORIES

Mrs X bought a nine-year-old TB gelding after a successful pre-purchase veterinary examination. Six months later, he was diagnosed as having navicular disease. The insurance company accepted that the interval between the pre-purchase examination and the diagnosis meant the condition could have developed after purchase, and agreed to pay.

Mrs Y's novice event horse strained a tendon and her vet told her that it was unlikely he would stand up to anything more than hacking in the future. Her insurers insisted on a period of rest and treatment before considering the claim, but Mrs Y wanted to replace the horse and had him destroyed. This made her claim invalid, as the insurance company had not given permission.

Safe and secure

Horse theft is one of those nightmares that you hope only happens to other people. Unfortunately, it is big business, as advertisements for missing animals prove. It is common sense to take every precaution; horse thieves, like burglars, look for easy pickings and every step you take to make things difficult for them safeguards your horse. Theft of tack and equipment is even more common: see page 150 for suggestions on how to protect yours.

One of the most vital basic steps is to make sure that you – and anyone else – can identify your horse. You might know him down to the last white marking and whorl, but to a non-horsy police officer a bay gelding is just another brown horse. A universally recognisable and visible identification is the best answer, which means freeze-marking and/or hoof branding.

With freeze-marking, it is essential that the company who marks the horse has an effective register and equally effective plan of action as soon as a horse goes missing.

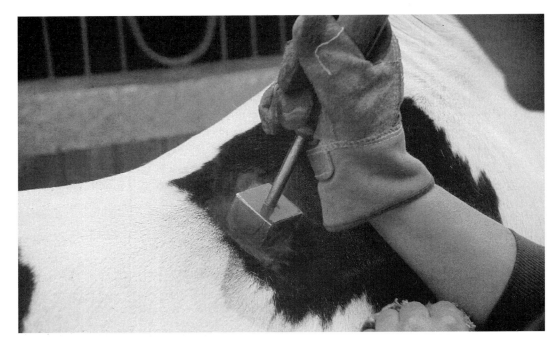

Freeze-marking is perhaps the most effective security measure you can take to protect your horse. Make sure the area is kept clipped so that the mark remains legible.

This means it must be able to liaise with police forces, ports, auctions and abattoirs. Road systems are now so good that a horse can be taken from one side of the country to the other before his owner realises that he is missing.

Some owners, particularly those who specialise in showing, dislike freeze-marking because they feel it is unsightly and that judges are prejudiced against it. As most horses can be marked in the saddle area, so that the mark is hidden when the horse is being ridden, the first argument is rather weak. It crumbles still farther if you ask someone whether he would rather see his horse every day with a freeze-mark or not see him at all because he has been stolen. The answer to the second point is that any judge who penalises a horse because of a freeze mark should not be judging at all: this one is fantasy rather than fact, or perhaps a convenient excuse for exhibitors who cannot accept that their horses are not as good as they think they are.

Hoof branding has been used by some army regiments and police forces for some-time, but is a comparatively recent commercial development. The most effective system, which has been patented by one company, utilises postcodes. Hoof branding must be carried out by a farrier; some farriers have complete sets of irons, or you can buy a set with your postcode and ask your farrier to apply them.

There are pros and cons with each identification system. Freeze-marking is permanent, but unsightly to some eyes, and if you have a grey or light coloured horse he may have to be marked on the shoulder rather than the saddle area. On dark coats, the hairs grow back white – with a grey, the irons have to be applied so that the hair does not grow back at all and the letters and numbers are actually areas of bare skin.

This could cause irritation under the saddle, so it is advised that such horses are marked on the shoulder or under the mane. The drawback to marking under the mane is that the mark is not always a visible deterrent, which is the main advantage of this system. Freeze-marks must be kept sharp and clear, which means clipping the area when winter coats become long and woolly. This is particularly important with 'bald' freeze-marks, as long hair may hide them.

Hoof brands may become covered up with mud during winter, so a thief may not realise at first that a horse is marked in this way. The brands also gradually grow out as the hoof grows down and have to be replaced – so in theory, although it is admittedly unlikely, a horse could be stolen and hidden away for several months until the hoof brands grew out.

Microchipping is another security system. There is no visible indication that a horse has been microchipped, which is either a disadvantage or an advantage, depending on your point of view! The only way to 'read' a microchip is via a special scanner, and as yet these are not used on as widespread a basis as might perhaps be ideal. If the day ever comes when every horse who passes through a sale ring, abattoir or port is automatically scanned, microchipping would win more devotees. As it is, some owners adopt a 'belt and braces' security system by having their animals both freeze-marked and microchipped.

None of these security measures are expensive, but there are other measures you can take which cost very little – or nothing at all. Steps to consider include:

- Take colour photographs of your horse in his winter and summer coat (clipped and unclipped, if appropriate). Take views from the front and from each side and pose him without a saddle or rider and so that all his markings can be seen. Your front view will show any head markings.
- Try and keep him at a place where someone lives on the premises. This helps to deter would-be thieves and means strange vehicles and disturbances are more likely to attract attention.
- Field gates which open directly on to a road make it easier for a thief to catch him, load him up and make a quick getaway. It is also easier to catch a horse who is wearing a headcollar, so unless it is absolutely essential, turn him out without one.
- Take the registration number of any strange vehicles parked near your yard or field or whose occupants seem to be taking an interest in the horses. It could be completely innocent, but then again, it might be someone working out the yard routine.
- Join your local Horsewatch scheme. Ask the crime prevention officer at your local police station to put you in touch with the nearest one – if it does not exist, discuss the possibility of starting one. This must only be done in conjunction with the police.

Tack theft is obviously less traumatic than horse theft, but it is bad enough. It is not just the annoyance of losing things you probably worked hard to pay for; dealing with administration necessary for police and insurance companies takes time and unless you can afford to replace essentials immediately, you may not be able to ride your horse until your insurance company pays out.

If you are not insured, the financial hardship is, of course, much worse. If you keep your tack at home, you should be covered on your household contents insurance: check your policy, as you may have to declare individual items separately on your proposal form if they are worth more than a certain amount.

In many ways, keeping your tack at home is safer than keeping it at a livery yard if you are able to transport it every time you ride. Some policies impose conditions that are downright impractical on most yards – for instance, one company insists that your tackroom must always be locked when your tack is in it. This is fine if you are the only rider, but often impossible when many owners are operating from the same yard.

Do not assume that you are automatically covered by your yard owner's insurance. Their policy will almost certainly cover only their own property, not that of their clients.

Police say that they often recover stolen saddlery, only to find that they cannot trace

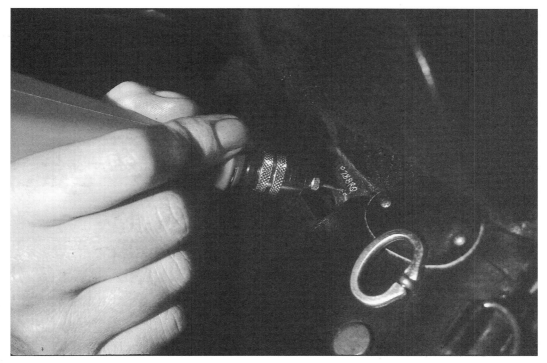

An inexpensive electric engraver can be used to mark metal fittings on tack – in this case, the stirrup bars on a saddle – with your postcode.

the rightful owner. Similarly, if your tack is stolen and you later recognise it at a sale – or even on someone else's horse – you will get nowhere if you cannot prove that it is yours. You might know that it is your saddle simply because you have ridden on it every day for the past three years, but you need more proof than that.

The answer is to note any existing identification marks, such as saddle serial numbers, and to mark everything you possess with your postcode. The most effective way is to use a metal engraver, which can be bought for about £25 – a small price compared to the value of your tack. Mark stirrup bars, buckles, bit rings and stirrup irons and do not forget rug buckles and surcingles.

It is also possible to mark leather with special ink which only shows up under ultra-violet light, but the ink gradually wears off and it is usually not satisfactory when leather is being cleaned regularly. Write your postcode in large letters on your rugs; even if they get partly obscured by dirt, it may deter someone from buying or using them.

As a burglary victim, I learned the hard way how difficult it is to remember every piece of horse equipment you have accumulated. Three weeks after filling in insurance details, I was remembering little things I had forgotten – a particular lead rope or even an expensive tub of ointment that was only remembered when it was needed.

Whilst life is too short to list every item you buy, it is worth making a list of what you already own and adding new items to it. It is also well worth taking colour photographs of saddles and bridles so that you have a record of their appearance and something to show a non-horsy police officer. If you have nothing to do with horses, they represent a foreign language full of Flashes, Grakles and drops.

The hardest decision

Having a horse put down is always an ordeal, particularly if the decision is not clearcut. If your horse has an accident and the attending vet tells you that on humane grounds, there is no alternative, then the decision is made for you. But when you are dealing with a horse who can no longer work, but for whom retirement is either not practical or not possible, it is a much harder one to make.

The most important yardstick is your horse's quality of life. If he can be kept comfortable and happy in retirement and you have the funds to make this feasible, then it is fair enough. But if he can only be kept 'paddock sound' on permanent medication, or if he is bored, you have to ask yourself if you are evading your responsibility.

With an old horse, it often helps to ask your vet's advice. If the horse's condition starts to deteriorate, you need to know where to draw the line between the inevitable progress of old age and the horse losing his quality of life.

You also have to make an honest appraisal of the sort of retirement you can provide for him. Retirement does not mean simply turning him out into a field and forgetting about him; he still needs worming, vaccinating, teeth rasping, regular attention from the farrier, shelter, feed, rugs . . . in fact, just about everything a working horse needs.

He also needs companionship, which means either keeping him where he can be turned out with other horses or finding him a home where he earns his keep as a companion to another horse. If you keep a horse at livery and hope to get another one, can you afford two lots of costs?

Even if you can find him a home as a companion, is his security guaranteed? For a start, most people want companion animals to be as cheap to keep as possible. If your horse is a 16.2hh Thoroughbred who needs lots of rugs, feed and stabling in winter, he may not be easy to place.

You may be lucky and find the perfect placement. But are you going to sell or give away the horse, in which case you have no control over his future and could take no action if, for instance, you discovered that he had been sold at auction a fortnight later? It sounds horrific, but some people are unscrupulous and it does happen.

If you safeguard against this happening by putting him on loan, with a written agreement, could you cope if you suddenly had to have him back in the middle of winter?

Again, these things happen: if your borrower is suddenly made redundant, or becomes seriously ill, an agreement may be impossible to enforce.

Nor can you expect one of the equine charities to take on your responsibilities for you. The established ones see their roles as re-homing horses to useful roles; acting as a companion animal may well be a useful role, but they are not in great demand. Even if a charity was prepared to help, you could find yourself being required to keep your horse until a place was available – which could be some time, as cases are assessed in terms of need.

The decision you make comes down to being honest with yourself. If you cannot guarantee your horse's future in every way, it may be kinder to have him put down: as a wise and compassionate horseman said to me when I was in this position, it is the last thing you can do for the horse you care about.

Practicalities

If your horse is put down, you have to decide who is going to do it, where it will happen, what method will be used and how the carcass will be disposed of afterwards. Because of their size, having a horse or pony put down is more complicated than with pets such as dogs and cats.

Those currently permitted to destroy horses are vets, licensed slaughterers (often called knackermen) and hunt kennelmen. Anyone who does the job has to make sure that arrangements have been made for disposal of the carcass: a vet will arrange for a knackerman to collect it whilst knackermen and hunts will deal with it.

Different people have different attitudes – many feel that the important thing is that the horse is put down as humanely as possible and that what happens afterwards is irrelevant. If you feel differently, there are commercial organisations offering cremation, though this is very expensive and you may feel that a more worthwhile way to remember your horse would be to make a donation in his memory to one of the welfare organisations. In some circumstances, it is possible for a horse to be buried on the owner's land, but there are rules about proximity to water courses that sometimes make it impossible.

Please do everything possible to make sure that your horse is put down in familiar surroundings. It may be upsetting for you, but he does not know what is going to happen and there is no risk that he will be excited or frightened by being taken some-where different. If for any reason this is impossible, licensed abattoirs will make an appointment for your horse to be taken there and put down immediately under veteri-nary supervision. Horses are dealt with by experienced handlers and surroundings are kept clean, but it has to be second best.

Finally, abattoirs will collect a horse, which must be the least satisfactory alterna-tive. When horses are put down at abattoirs it is usually for commercial reasons, so that the owner can recoup the carcass money. This depends on type and size and averages £300, as long as there has been a sufficient withdrawal period from drugs which would render the carcass useless. A financial consideration of this kind does not usually apply to the private owner. If the horse is put down at home, you may have to pay a small amount for disposal.

There are two methods of humane destruction, shooting and lethal injection. When the first is carried out properly it is instantaneous and the horse is dead before he hits the ground. Although a vet should do the job perfectly competently, many people prefer to use a knackerman purely because he will be used to handling horses and is doing it all the time – which hopefully does not apply to your vet. The knackermen I have met have all been caring men who like horses; it may seem to be a contradiction in terms, but as one put it, 'It's a job that has to be done and someone has to do it.'

Shooting is inevitably noisy and there is usually involuntary movement after the horse is dead. It is necessary for someone to hold the horse; some owners want to be with their horse to the end but it is not a responsibility to enter into lightly. For the horse's sake, it is vital that everyone concerned stays calm, and it is difficult if not impossible to guarantee this when you are upset. It is far better to find someone prepared to help: if given warning, your vet or the knackerman may be able to bring an assistant.

Euthanasia by intravenous injection takes longer and some horses may fight the effect of the drugs. The best policy is to discuss all the options with your vet when possible so that you are aware of the pros and cons in your particular circumstances.

When it's all over...

If you are fond of your horse, having him put down is distressing even when you know that it is the right decision. As with any loss, it is important to allow yourself to grieve.

If it is a decision that has taken a long time to reach, do not feel guilty for feeling relieved that it has actually happened. Some people want to look for another horse straight away, but in most cases it is better to allow time for your emotions to settle down and for you to get used to what has happened.

Do not be surprised if you have moments of doubt and start asking yourself if there was something else you could have done. You may also have to cope with unthinking and sometimes unbelievable remarks from other people. I once had a much loved horse put down after we had tried for a year to rehabilitate him after a sacroiliac injury; my vet, one of the top horse vets in the country, said there was nothing else we could do and the horse was unhappy doing nothing. An acquaintance told me that she thought I was stupid having him put down when such a good looking animal would have fetched a good thousand pounds in a sale, even unwarranted!

When the time comes to look for another horse, try and think in terms of finding a horse you will enjoy riding and be able to build a new partnership with, rather than of looking for a replacement for your previous one. Animals are individuals just as much as people are, and whilst you may have a preference for a particular type or breed, it is a mistake to assume that the same qualities will always apply.

Nor is it necessarily a good idea to look for a completely different type of horse. If you think that you would like to change course, try and ride as many different types as possible before you start reading the adverts – preferably by asking friends to let you try their horses, rather than looking at horses for sale when you have no idea what you are looking for.

At first, you may feel as if you could not cope with owning a horse again. Some owners stick to that decision, at least for a while. But for most of us, horses are such an important part of our lives that the gap they leave is too large to ignore.

Give yourself time, and you will remember the good bits as well as the bad. A bright, clear day will leave you wishing you could ride . . . not just any horse, but a horse of your own. An advert for a show, an instructional clinic or a sponsored ride will make you want to be back in the swing of things.

Surviving as a horse owner is not just about getting through the difficult, time-consuming, expensive bits. It is also about making the most of the good things – and there are plenty of them, even when the going gets tough.

Index